Diane

Caustic quotes

An A-Z of quotes, insults and one-liners

Helen Ingram

Gap Publishing

CAUSTIC QUOTES

Published in 2002 by
Gap Publishing
44 Wendell Street, Norman Park
Queensland 4170, Australia

Cover design by John Braben
Formatting by Post Pre Press Group

Printed in Australia by
McPherson's Printing Group

ISBN 0 947163 53 0

Contents

FAMILY:

GOVERNMENT:

HARMONY:

HEALTH:

IDEOLOGY:

Action

Action

Not even a mosquito gets a slap on the back until it starts working.

Either lead, follow or get out of the way.

If you can't move the mountain, tunnel through.

By all means keep your feet firmly on the ground, but keep them moving.

The best course of action is always determined by subsequent events.

After you talk the talk, you have to walk the walk.

Action removes the doubt that theory cannot resolve.

What doesn't squeak, doesn't get oiled.

The smallest deed achieves more than the greatest intention.

There are two types, the doers and those who wonder why it wasn't done their way.

God helps those who are willing to work.

Some make it happen, some watch, and some wonder what happened.

If you're still talking about what you did yesterday, you haven't done much today.

You miss every single shot you were too afraid to take.

Big words seldom lead to big deeds.

Give me a place to stand, and I will move the earth.

People react to people who act.

Pay no attention to what people say, watch what they do.

You achieve nothing by turning an idea over in your mind.

Action defines us as much as we define our actions.

Don't drift or drop anchor. Sail, against the wind.

If you live in the valley, don't annoy those who live on the hill.

Action overwhelms nature's silence.

A journey of a thousand miles begins with a single step.

He who hesitates is last because he looks before he leaps.

Seize the opportunity while the path remains lit.

Desire is the source of all action.

To move a mountain, start by removing a single pebble.

Sit back and take what comes, or go after what you want.

Your food is near your stomach, but it can't get there by itself.

Sometimes men of action are too busy to see beyond that day's work.

If you think you can't, you're probably right.

No motive, no action, no result.

Ideas don't work unless you make them.

When you're confronted by a deadly snake, you don't pause to wonder where he came from.

Everyone complains about the weather, but no-one does anything except criticise it.

The best time to do it is between yesterday and tomorrow.

Use it before you lose it.

If you have an itch for success, scratch it.

When your horse is running well, don't stop to offer it sugar.

Ugly deeds breed ugly deeds.

If you want something done, ask a busy man. The others have no time.

Think slowly then act quickly.

Consequences

Take away the cause, and the effect ceases.

The planter swore his rows were straight, but the seeds knew better.

If you can't face the music, you'll never lead the band.

You only fall off the bicycle if you stop pedalling.

A life without cause is a life without effect.

Your pebble also makes ripples in other people's ponds.

The consequences of anger are often worse than the cause of it.

Your thoughtless actions can change someone else's life forever.

The lone snowflake never believes it contributed to the avalanche.

The means determines the end.

We worry about what a child might become, forgetting what he already is.

Cause and effect are the flip sides of a single fact.

Once you've pulled the trigger, the bullet doesn't stop until it reaches it's destination.

Good swimmers are more likely to drown, because they take more chances.

Venus de Milo bit her nails.

Control your emotion, or it will control you.

The fruit pre-exists in the seed.

What goes up, must come down.

You can dodge responsibility, but not it's consequences.

A heavy burden doesn't always kill on the day it is carried.

If you hang onto a tiger's tail, sooner or later you have to let go.

Action is the basic cause of all effects.

Suppose Noah had missed the boat?

When you stop trying to be someone else, you become someone.

You can't unscramble scrambled eggs.

Good intentions sometimes turn out badly, and bad intentions sometimes turn out well.

Laughter cannot bring back what anger has chased away.

The inept always intended to do what someone else just completed.

When a horse shakes it's tail, flies disperse.

They have sown the wind, and they will reap the whirlwind.

Sour grapes never make sweet wine.

Do your best. Do your best. Do your best. Well done.

Nothing comes from nothing.

The bee that collects the pollen makes the honey.

One thing leads to another.

The cause is often hidden, but the effects are visible.

It goes, it comes back.

What's done is done, repent it as you may.

Don't throw the old bucket out before you know if the new one leaks.

Don't forget the diver, every penny makes the water warmer.

You reap what you sow.

The caravan doesn't stop because little dogs bark.

Clapping with the right hand produces no noise.

It's no good crying over spilt milk, especially if you put in all in one can.

The source of the fire isn't important until the flames are out.

Effort

Effort only rewards those who refuse to quit.

You can't drag your feet if you're pulling your weight.

If you give up before you succeed, how does anyone know you tried?

If at first you don't succeed, just keep flogging the dead horse.

The best place to find a helping hand is at the end of your arm.

He who limps is still walking by himself.

If you must be bad, be the very worst you can be.

Those that don't work, always know of a scheme that does.

I'll get what I want, even if I have to detour through hell to get to it.

You can be on the right track, but you'll still get run over if you just stand there.

Just begin at the beginning, go on to the middle, and stop when you get to the end.

The sun loses nothing by shining into a puddle.

The greater the obstacle, the more glory in overcoming it.

If things don't go according to plan, maybe it's because there was no plan.

If you don't execute good ideas, they die by themselves.

Plant nothing, nothing grows.

The best time to tackle a small problem is before it gets any bigger.

If at first you don't succeed, redefine success.

Just do it.

Nothing is easy for the unwilling.

The road to success is named Perseverance.

I will not retreat until I have been heard.

You can't make an omelette without breaking eggs.

Put your best foot forward, but don't step on anyone's toes.

Failure is the path of least persistence.

If in doubt, make it sound convincing.

The compass points the way, but you have to make the journey.

Whatever you find hardest to do, do with all your might.

A sharp axe and a strong arm fell the tallest tree.

Great works are performed not by strength but by perseverance.

Ideas don't work unless you do.

The secret of success is consistency of purpose.

The best preparation for work is work.

If we could do everything twice, it would be better the second time around.

No matter how hard you try, I still find you very trying.

Looking for trouble is a waste of time, it will find you soon enough.

Much effort, much prosperity.

There's a direct link between what you put in and what you get out.

The time will come when you will hear of me, for I will never give up.

If you want the fruit, you have to climb the tree.

You can talk yourself into anything.

I'm not sure where I'm going, but I'm halfway there.

It's amazing what you can achieve if you don't care who gets the credit.

You have to be able to admit that you're not building a mound, but digging a pit.

You never know what you can do until you try.

The difference between a rut and a grave is their dimensions.

Limitations

Not every oyster contains a pearl.

The ground covered by the rider is limited to the speed of the horse.

Owning a piano doesn't make you a pianist.

Trying to teach a pig to sing is a waste of your time, and it annoys the pig.

You can only dream one dream at a time.

Even when a dwarf stands on a mountain, he's still a dwarf.

The potential for honey lies in each flower, but it takes a honey bee to release it.

I'd give my right arm to be ambidextrous.

You cannot drive straight on a twisting road.

Better one sure method than a hundred uncertainties.

If you can't ride two horses at the same time, you shouldn't be in the circus.

Eagles don't catch flies.

There's no point in giving a man in the middle of the Sahara a wine list.

Sometimes a swallow builds its nest on a tent.

If you fight fire with fire, you end up with ashes.

Don't bite the hand that feeds the goose that lays the golden egg.

A tough log needs a tough wedge.

Sometimes high standards are just an excuse to absolve possible failure.

If we accept the prevailing standards, it's because we have none of our own.

You can't light a fire with a wet match.

No bird soars too high with its own wings.

That's as effective as trying to blow out a light bulb.

What seems vital today may not even be desirable tomorrow.

The king's palace is not the place to pick a fight with the king.

You can't hatch chickens from fried eggs.

Sometimes it's a case of the tail wagging the dog.

A wolf cannot lead two packs at the same time.

No stream rises higher than its source.

If you can't stand the heat, get out of the kitchen.

It's like asking a blind man to show you the way.

That's as useful as sending a kiss by messenger.

You will eventually be assimilated into what you resist.

Never negotiate out of fear, or fear to negotiate.

As useful as putting horseshoes on a goose.

Don't keep a dog and bark yourself.

I would rather ride a donkey that carries me than a horse that throws me.

It's like giving a starving man a toothpick.

There's not much point in writing in a chimney with charcoal.

As much use as sawing sawdust.

He's an eight ulcer man doing a four ulcer job.

While everyone praises the peacock's feathers, it cries about its ugly feet.

There's not much of a choice between rotten apples.

That's as useful as using a guillotine to cure dandruff.

The best brewer sometimes makes bad beer.

The best flower beds sometimes have weeds.

You don't need an axe to break open an egg.

Age

Youth

Teenagers can be nice sometimes, but they recover quickly.

Teenagers are just like other people, but with a bad attitude.

Between the ages of twelve to seventeen, a parent ages thirty years.

It's not what teenagers know that worries parents, it's how they found out.

There's nothing wrong with teenagers that telling them won't aggravate.

Never forget that you're dealing with a sensitive little bastard.

A teenager stops asking where it came from and refuses to say where it's going.

Puberty is when a child discovers love is a weapon he can use against his parents.

Consent, dissent, resent.

Society gets the teenagers it deserves.

They have it all, but they don't know how to use any of it.

A teenager is a minor with a major attitude.

Be nice to your kids, because one day they'll get to choose your nursing home.

Today's youth are the trustees of tomorrow's history.

Never lend your car to anyone you have given birth to.

To keep teenagers at home, be kind and pleasant, and barricade them in.

It's not true what people say. Many parents are very obedient.

The man with a full set of tools has no sons.

A wild young colt can be born of an old nag.

Never allow your children to ask what's for dinner unless they intend to make it.

Teenagers are God's punishment for having sex.

As soon as they get old enough to help around the house, they leave.

Ask a teenager, because they think they know everything.

Puberty is when parents start worrying about pregnancy all over again.

The only person not awed by the lion tamer is the school bus driver.

She shops, therefore she is.

A delinquent is someone who does exactly what his parents used to do.

Youth is a series of eruptions, followed by the silent treatment.

Teenagers complain that there's nothing to do, but they stay out all night doing it.

The one thing you rarely see in a teenager's room is the floor.

Teenagers get the telephone calls, parents get the telephone bills.

The fact that teenagers grow into adults is a tribute to their parents' self control.

Age is best measured by events, not by years.

Adolescence is when a girl's voice changes from no to yes.

Babysitting is when a teenager acts like an adult, so that the adults can go out and act like teenagers.

We have enough youth, how about a fountain of smart?

Youth is when you realise your parents were still around when the dinosaurs died.

First they love you, then they judge you, but they rarely forgive you.

They never raised a hand against any of their children, except in self defence.

Teenagers are very unpleasant when you get to No them.

Teenagers need their parents. Who else would get so upset at being ignored?

Middle Age

Middle age is when Father Time starts catching up with Mother Nature.

Once you're over the hill, you pick up speed.

I know I'm in the prime of life, I just wish it didn't take so long to get primed.

If we improve the older we get, I must be approaching magnificent.

Middle age is when your get up and go has got up and gone.

You're only as old as you feel the next day.

Wrinkles are a sign from God that your days are numbered.

Middle age is when beauty moves from your face to your heart.

If I'd known I was going to live this long, I would have taken better care of my body.

If I had to have wrinkles, why couldn't they be on the bottom of my feet?

Life is finally going my way, but I'd rather stay at home.

Middle age is when you can make a fool of yourself in a far more dignified way.

She's not pushing forty, she's been dragging it behind her for years.

I had a magnificent body before it went in for a career of its own.

Age leaves more wrinkles on the soul than on the face.

Middle age is when a narrow waist and a broad mind change places.

The secret to staying young is to eat right, exercise, and lie about your age.

When you're middle aged you go to seed, but when you're young you go to pot.

Most of us spend the first half of our lives making the second half miserable.

Old age is fifteen years older than I am.

Few women admit their age, few men act theirs.

I intend to take my time getting to fifty.

You're only young once, but you can be immature forever.

I didn't stop playing because I got old, I got old because I stopped playing.

Age is a bad travelling companion.

She has discovered the secret of perpetual middle age.

Middle age is when you stop criticising the older generation and start criticising the younger one.

I own underwear older than my children.

She is fifty, trying hard to be thirty.

We separate more distinctly and connect more closely.

Growing old isn't so bad when you consider the alternative.

Middle age is when you finally admit it didn't get lost, but that you lost it.

Life begins at forty, just as the body begins to wear out.

Middle age is when you feel like a colt and look like an old nag.

She overstayed forty.

At about thirty five, something terrible happens to music.

Middle age is when you still think you'll feel better in the morning.

I've still got everything I had twenty years ago, only it hangs a little lower now.

Revenge is sweet. Live long enough to be a burden to your children.

You're getting old when you've given up all your bad habits and you still feel terrible.

Middle age is when you exchange admiring glances for pitying looks.

By fifty you know what you want to be - twenty five again.

Middle age is that time when your age begins to show around your middle.

The good old days always seem better because we were younger then.

She claims she's approaching forty. From which direction?

Old Age

I finally got it all together, but I can't remember where I put it.

When Mozart was my age, he'd already been dead for a year.

The older a man gets, the higher he could jump as a young man.

What doesn't ache, doesn't work.

If you make it to a hundred and five, you've got it made. No-one dies after that.

It's the metallic age, gold in the teeth, silver in the hair and lead in the pants.

Old age is the destination in the journey from compassion to apathy.

It's not old age that's devastating, it's the side effects.

All of a sudden old people are the same age as me.

May the Lord love us, but not call us too soon.

Just because there's snow on the roof, doesn't mean there's no fire in the hearth.

Old people weigh more because of the extra knowledge they carry.

You know you're getting old when the candles cost more than the birthday cake.

It's terrible growing old alone, my wife hasn't had a birthday in years.

When we're young, we shed tears without grief, and when we're old, we grieve without tears.

Old age is when getting ahead means just keeping up.

Forty is the old age of youth, fifty is the youth of old age.

Young folk, silly folk. Old folk, cold folk.

By the time you decide to watch your step, you're too old to go anywhere.

Age before beauty, pearls before swine.

They tried to count the candles, but the heat drove them back.

At one point, old age, all diseases merge.

There's many a good tune played on an old fiddle.

Youth without fire is like old age without experience.

A man is only as old as the woman he feels.

Old age is when you've learned it all, but you can't remember any of it.

I am in the prime of senility.

May you live to be a hundred and have an extra year to repent.

There's not much future in old age.

Now that I've learned to make the most of it, there's not much of it left.

Old age is when the candles cost more than the cake.

When I grow up again, I want to be a little boy.

The secret of longevity is bread, but you have to eat it for at least a hundred years.

You really want to give that pregnant woman your seat, but you just can't get up.

Old people are prickly because when rose petals fall, all that's left is the thorns.

You're not old until your age becomes an excuse to give up your goals.

It's when you know all the answers and nobody asks you the questions.

Old age forbids, upon pain of death, the pleasures of youth.

No-one loves life as much as an old man.

When the snake is old, the frog will tease him.

The young suffer less from their own errors than they do from the caution of the old.

Wrinkles are long service stripes earned in the hard campaign of life.

Today an altar cloth, tomorrow a rag.

The worst aspect of growing old is having to listen to advice from your children.

He who clings to youth is not a perpetual young man but an old boy.

Ancestry

Ancestry

Scratch an ancestor, and a skeleton falls out of the closet.

Never forget that we're all descended from Adam and Eve, who lived naked in someone's garden before they were evicted for stealing apples.

Taking pride in your ancestors is like looking forward to the past.

A good family tree is useful only for social climbing.

Of course my family didn't come over with the first settlers, they were already here waiting to greet the new arrivals.

Only stupid people confine themselves to the limits set by their ancestors.

God created man because he was disappointed in the monkey.

The purest blood in the world is carried by mosquitoes and the blood bank.

Many a family tree would be better used for firewood.

Even the best ancestry can still only be traced back to an ape.

You are the sap of your family tree.

Let the dead bury the dead.

Progress is one step forward and two steps backwards.

Why do people keep trying to reform their ancestors?

The royal family's ancestors included traitors, adulterers and murderers.

You won't find your place in the sun by sitting in the shade of the family tree.

To get ahead, you need something to leave behind.

The certainties of one age are the problems of the next.

Pride is all that's left over from rich ancestors after the money has been spent.

Every generation revolts against its parents and embraces its grandparents.

To get ahead, you must have something to run away from.

They can't pay what we owed, so why do some of us assume their debts?

Some people can trace their family tree back to the time they lived in it.

A mule is without pride of ancestry or hope of posterity.

Ancestry may be advanced, but we each begin afresh.

The best portion of ancestors is underground.

We are wise with the wisdom of our times, and ignorant with its ignorance.

The egg is the source of it all.

Boasting about ancestors means you belong to a family that's better dead than alive.

Amongst the dead are those who still haven't been allowed to die.

Don't follow in their footsteps, seek new paths as they did.

Misers make the best ancestors.

People without talent boast about their ancestors.

Ancestry is a drama with an interesting past.

We pay for our ancestors' indiscretions, even if they didn't leave us any money.

A genealogist traces back your family tree as far as your money will go.

The wisdom of our ancestors went no further than they did.

Don't condemn your ancestors, they had no choice either.

If we're descended from monkeys, haven't we done well?

The novelties of the new generation are the resuscitated fashions of the past.

They live on by leaping over oblivion into succeeding generations.

Heredity

Heredity is the point at which the past and the present meet.

If your parents never had it, you won't either.

The first generation plants the tree, and the next generation sits in its shade.

Everyone has to do their own growing, no matter how tall their parents were.

We are our re-animated ancestors.

The certainties of one age are the problems of the next.

Every tree has roots.

It's not what you inherit from your ancestors, it's what you bequeath your descendants.

Pride yourself on your own virtues.

No child is responsible for his father. That's his mother's affair.

We resemble our environment more than we resemble our forefathers.

The glory of our ancestors in no way reflects our abilities.

The king never dies.

Nothing enhances the abilities of an ancestor more than a talented child.

The best pedigrees belong to those who are so inbred that they're unfit for breeding.

The law of heredity is that all the undesirable traits come from the other parent.

An ape is an ape, even if you dress it in silk.

What it lacks in height, it makes up for in length.

It isn't easy to take the salt out of sea water.

Celibacy is not an inherited trait.

Breeding isn't everything, but it is fun.

Old sins cast long shadows.

Bad hen, bad egg.

The child is the father of the man.

If we thought we would live forever, we wouldn't care about our offspring.

Ancestry is a hereditary condition.

Descendants are ancestors' history rewritten.

Celibacy is not hereditary.

A tree is known by its fruit.

Blood is destiny.

Teenagers undermine parents' belief in heredity.

Madness is hereditary, you get it from your children.

It runs in the family.

A ferocious eagle does not father a timid dove.

We come into the world marked by our descent.

Never shake the family tree too hard, you never know what may fall out.

If a cat gives birth to a kitten in a stove, are the offspring biscuits?

What is inbred in the bone is present in the flesh.

Show me a hero and I will write you a tragedy.

We are our own ancestors.

The father's nature lies dormant in the infant.

Life and death are hereditary.

What does it matter who your grandfather was? What matters is who his grandson is.

That which comes of a cat will want to catch mice.

Good seed makes a good crop.

Heredity relieves us of the responsibility for our own shortcomings.

Animosity

Anger

We all boil at different degrees.

The more arguments you win, the lonelier you get.

Keep giving people a piece of your mind, and soon you won't have any of it left.

Why go to bed angry, when you can stay up and fight?

Keep your temper. I don't want it.

It's better to debate without deciding, than to decide without debating.

If I didn't understand you so well, I wouldn't disagree with you so much.

If you're arguing with a fool, he's doing the same thing.

You learn nothing from people who agree with you.

It infuriates me to be wrong when I know I'm right.

If you're about to hit the ceiling, make sure the shit hasn't already hit the fan.

If I've said anything to offend you, please believe me.

A silent person hasn't necessarily been converted.

As it's used up, anger replenishes itself.

The less there is in the pot, the quicker it boils.

An angry person is surrounded by angry people.

Later, all the clever retorts we could have made come back to haunt us.

No-one ever tells me anything until I contradict them.

Some potentially good arguments get ruined by people who know what they're talking about.

Anger is the honesty of the heart breaking free of the prison of the head.

Anger makes the mouth work faster than the mind.

Any stigma will serve to beat a dogma.

A hot temper easily leaps over a cold resolution.

It takes forty muscles to frown, but only ten to punch someone.

Anger erupts through the mouth while the brain is busy smouldering.

If you strike in anger, you miss the mark.

If you've got a screw loose, you'll fly off the handle.

Anger feeds on itself.

No-one wants to argue with me, just because I'm always right.

Nothing lowers the level of a conversation more than raising the voice.

Anger is fanned by words.

Never argue at the dinner table, the hungry person always loses.

What you say when you're angry is the best speech you'll ever regret.

A dog is a four legged animal provided by God for man to kick when things go wrong.

You can't express love with a clenched fist.

Make a man angry in argument, and you have overcome him.

When angry, count four, when very angry, swear.

Blow a fuse and you'll be left in the dark.

There's no such thing as a convincing argument.

What goes up must come down, remember that when you fly into a rage.

An angry man rides a horse that runs away with him.

Never try to bring a man down to earth at the height of his rage.

Anger punishes another while torturing itself.

Criticism

A critic is a nasty little parasite who lives off the efforts of others.

If you're continually running someone down, you're not moving forward yourself.

I would rather be ruined by praise than saved by criticism.

Any old vulture can find a carcass.

The aim of criticism should be progress, not victory.

Criticism is a big bite, usually out of someone's back.

A critic takes infinite pains and gives them to someone else.

Good is never good enough when better is expected.

Destruction is the trade of those who don't know how to build.

When I criticise you it's constructive, when you criticise me, it's destructive.

My worst fault is that I'm too critical of myself.

To criticise is to knock without entering.

Don't fix the blame, fix the problem.

Sometimes the squeaky wheel is the one that gets replaced.

You can't turn an argument upside down if you don't know which is the right way up.

If it isn't perfect, make it better.

Don't worry, he's only trying to cut you down to his size.

He says what he means, and he usually means something nasty.

Criticism from a wise man is better than the enthusiastic approval of a fool.

A critic doesn't want to kill you, he just likes to see you bleed.

Better a flawed diamond than a perfect pebble.

He has the irritating habit of looking for a flaw in any argument.

He's always hovering about, waiting to be offended.

A critic dismisses a hen's style, without knowing how to lay an egg himself.

He looks for faults as though they were buried treasure.

Those who cannot perform condemn those who can.

It's easy to criticise others, which is why we all do it.

Criticism is prejudice made plausible.

A critic is someone who suffers from twenty-twenty hindsight.

If you want to beat a dog, you're bound to find a stick.

A critic can drive the car, but he doesn't know the way.

Suicide is the most severe form of self-criticism.

A critic will even find fault with heaven.

If you're afraid of criticism, you'll die doing nothing.

Even a broken watch is right twice a day.

When critics disagree, the artist is in accord with himself.

A whip raises welts but a tongue can crush.

Remember, your wife's faults are what stopped her from getting a better husband.

Critics are only hard to please because no-one wants to please them.

Switching off someone else's torch won't make yours shine brighter.

It's easier to criticise an egg than to lay one.

Censors are grubby little people who get to see smutty movies first.

A critic rips apart what he cannot construct.

Enemies

Love your enemies, it drives them nuts.

You'll never be your own worst enemy while I'm alive.

Forget your enemies, it's the friends you annoy that cause problems.

Friends come and go, but enemies last a lifetime.

He has a heart of gold, but so has a hard boiled egg.

A dead enemy never stinks.

Money can't buy you friends, but it raises the class of enemy you make.

Pay attention to your enemies, they're the first to discover your mistakes.

I'd flatten you, but shit splatters.

Smile at your enemy, it cons him into coming closer so that you can thump him.

If you have no enemies, you haven't lived.

He who loves his enemies, betrays his friends.

You can meet friends anywhere, but you have to make enemies.

A common danger unites the bitterest enemies.

The most potent enemy is the ex-friend, because he knows precisely where to strike.

You make enemies by constantly complaining to friends.

Any impartial person can clearly see that I am never in the wrong.

Enemies are proof that you stood for something.

Laughing at your own mistakes lengthens your life, laughing at mine shortens it.

You can't be too careful about your choice of enemies.

Guard your enemy's rights, or set a precedent that will ultimately apply to you.

We provide our enemies with the means of our own destruction.

Scratch a discarded lover, and you find an enemy.

Silence makes no enemies.

Our friends, the enemy.

Enemies hate you, in spite of your virtues.

A wise man gets more use out of his enemies than a fool gets out of his friends.

He doesn't have a single enemy in the world, and none of his friends like him either.

You don't have to love your enemies, just treat your friends better.

Since I wronged you, I've always disliked you.

Speak well of your enemies, remember you made them yourself.

Nothing annoys an enemy as much as being forgiven.

If there is no enemy within, the enemy without doesn't really matter.

If our enemies limped, it would be easier to recognise them.

There are times when I don't even agree with myself.

Real antagonism is love which hasn't recognised itself.

The worse the offence, the less likely the offender is to forgive you.

Be happy, and make sure your enemies know it.

He who cannot agree with his enemies is controlled by them.

Never judge a man by what his enemies say about him.

You can judge a man by his enemies as well as his friends.

You are the only reason why your enemy can't become a friend.

Some enemies disguise themselves as friends.

Your worst enemy can become your best friend once he's underground.

Even if your enemy is as insignificant as an ant, treat him as though he was an elephant.

Hatred

Everybody doesn't hate you, everybody doesn't know you.

You don't even have a single redeeming defect.

There's no viper so little that it doesn't have venom.

Hatred is anger that has had an opportunity to develop.

You're only alive because it's illegal for me to kill you.

It's better to be hated for what you are, than to be loved for what you are not.

May a band of gypsies camp in your belly and teach bears to dance on your liver.

I like nasty people because it removes the need to dislike them before you hate them.

Hatred is a tonic that inspires us to live long enough to exact vengeance.

You should always hate someone, just to keep your discrimination bright.

Love soon turns to indifference, but when indifference becomes hatred, it lasts forever.

Hatred corrodes the soul.

Love is often false, but hatred is without hypocrisy.

I wouldn't pee down your throat if your lungs were on fire.

Hey Stupid, why does everyone hate me?

It's easy to stop hating someone, but only after you get even.

You are like two buttocks on one bum.

I don't hate my enemies, but I'm pleased when God makes them look riciulous.

Hatred is the longest lasting of all the emotions.

I once loved you too much not to hate you now.

Self-indulgence is the shortest route to hatred.

You could suck an egg out of a chicken.

My enemies' hatred has shown me what I am.

Hatred is the most enduring human passion.

Men love in haste, but they hate at leisure.

Hatred is like burning down your house to get rid of a rat.

What we fear most, we grow to hate.

Hatred is a heart infection.

I admire a good hater.

You are a dung beetle that owes its existence to animal droppings.

Anyone can love, but hatred is an art.

You are the justification needed for euthanasia.

Excessive hatred of evil distorts your vision of goodness.

There is no cure for hatred.

When you are hated, both your good and bad deeds oppress you.

The price of hating someone else is loving ourselves.

If looks could kill, I'd have a nasty bruise.

Hatred provides the most enduring pleasure.

I've always hated you and I always will.

Hate is the number between seven and nine.

The goodness of our enemies only makes us hate them more.

Hatred is the most consuming illness of our times.

I'm looking at you, despite the effort.

Hatred eats you from the inside outwards.

What we cannot identify with disturbs us, and what disturbs us, we ultimately hate.

When you hate someone, even their virtues become ugly blemishes.

Revenge

One good kick deserves another.

Revenge is delicious, but it must be left to ripen.

If the state won't punish you, I will.

To seek revenge gives us a purpose in life.

Do me wrong, and dare to sleep.

Two wrongs are the beginning of a feud.

If your enemy wrongs you, buy each of his children a drum.

I wish all your teeth would fall out, except for one, which had terrible toothache.

Revenge will be revenged.

I wanted to make a fool out of you, but nature beat me to it.

Revenge tears your own wounds open.

Use your enemy's kindness as fuel against him.

Don't get mad, get even.

Malice swallows the greater part of its own venom.

To have a grievance gives us a purpose in life.

May the skin of your bum one day cover a drum.

To err is human, to get even feels divine.

A woman's desire for revenge outlasts all her other emotions.

Revenge prevents wounds from healing.

It's like burning down your own house so that your mother-in-law can't stay over.

Forgetting is a mild form of revenge.

You have to do him before he do you.

Revenge is profitable, gratitude is expensive.

Those who seek revenge are mental invalids, the walking wounded.

Revenge is the poor delight of little minds.

You pay for revenge with a piece of your soul.

If prayer fails, get help to get even.

I cannot be revenged thanks to my enemy, but I owe it to myself never to forget.

When the cat dies, the mice rejoice.

Neglect will kill an injury sooner than revenge.

Living well is the best revenge.

Revenge is a more punctual paymaster than gratitude.

Revenge emanates from a soul in pain.

Blood cannot be washed out with blood.

Ask only how you can get back at them.

No matter how well you nurse a grudge, it just gets sicker and sicker.

Revenge is a dish best served cold.

Do as you are done by.

If you plant thorns, don't expect to harvest rose petals.

He who makes a curse will surely suffer because of that curse.

Revenge is its own executioner.

Revenge is a fire so hot that no-one can touch it without getting their own fingers burnt.

You can't get ahead if you're trying to get even.

Revenge is sweet, but not when you're on the receiving end.

Revenge feeds off despair.

You pay for revenge with a piece of your soul.

Appearance

Appearance

Everything she has is in the window display, but the shop has no stock.

Things are seldom what they seem, skim milk masquerades as cream.

The eyes have a single language world wide.

Physical features are merely permanent gestures.

You too could have a body like mine, but it doesn't come cheap.

Those who lack good looks, more than compensate with personality.

An untainted soul often lives in a warped body.

One look at her, and you realise God has a sense of humour after all.

She's not bad looking, if you like the type.

He has a good head on his shoulders, but no neck.

That which is not apparent outside, is apparent within.

You can't do anything about the face, but you can control the expression on it.

She spends hours at the beauty salon, just getting an estimate.

She's blonde, dyed by her own hand.

The nanny is an animated adenoid.

If your face is your fortune, you've had a hard life.

Only shallow people pretend not to judge others by appearance.

A beautiful heart often hides in an ordinary body.

With a face like that, it's better to sneak up on the mirror.

If the beard was everything, a goat could preach.

Not every person a dog barks at is a thief.

Mick Jagger has child-bearing lips.

His features don't know the value of teamwork.

Those ears make him look like a taxi with both doors open.

She's a fallen angel, too bad she landed on her face.

We value people for what they seem to be.

You can see a person's face, but not their mind.

It's not so much the face as the expression on it.

Wearing a beret doesn't make you French.

She has a sympathetic face. One look at her, and everyone is sympathetic.

Never judge a man by the size of his car.

That's not a model, it's a terrible example.

His right eye is fascinating, the left one keeps looking at it.

A man's face is an autobiography, a woman's face is a work of fiction.

All that glitters is not gold.

Michael Jackson has had so much cosmetic surgery that when he blinks, his left leg lifts.

This is a face filled with broken commandments.

My face is my chaperone.

Stevie Wonder smiles all the time because he doesn't know how ugly he is.

When he was circumcised, the rabbi threw the wrong part away.

She looks like Hitler, but without the moustache.

A wolf looks like a dog.

The money looks the same, but inflation has diminished its value.

Never judge a man's actions before you know his motives.

Baldness

I could tell you things about baldness that would make your hair fall out.

I bet you're wondering if I'm bald everywhere.

The problem isn't production, it's distribution.

It's not a bald patch, it's a solar panel for a love machine.

Bald heads are beautiful. God covered the ugly ones with hair.

Every time I plucked a grey hair, ten thousand others went to its funeral.

My baldness is a disguise. I'm working undercover.

Hair doesn't fall out, it falls in and later re-emerges through the ears and nose.

Virility makes your hair fall out.

A skinhead is a cheap imitation of the truly magnificent natural bald.

When God takes away hair, he bestows intelligence.

I may not be well endowed with hair, but I more than compensate in other ways.

Dandruff used to be a thrill.

I'm bald because I don't have the time to listen to a barber give me a haircut.

Barbers make cutting remarks.

It falls out faster than it grows.

The only thing that got thinner as I got older was my hair.

You cannot cure grief by pulling your hair out.

When the wind blows, a bald man only has to straighten his tie.

His hair has departed in the middle.

Baldness is never burdened with superfluous parts.

It's not so much that I'm bald, it's that everyone else is so hairy.

My head sadly lacks short cuts.

A hat is the best cure for baldness.

Bald heads are so full of brains that there's no room for hair follicles.

The very hairs on your head are numbered.

At last, I'm in style.

Why are bald men so sensitive about their hair when they don't have any?

It's hard to get ahead if you don't have one.

There is nothing worse than a man who pretends to have hair.

When you're bald, your hair is always neat.

The less hair you have, the more face there is to wash.

No bald man was ever convinced of an argument during the fly season.

A bald man will never be grey.

To a bald man, grey hair looks wonderful.

Never ask a barber if you need a haircut.

Hair breeds vanity.

A bald man is the first one to know when it starts to rain.

It could be worse. Imagine if it ached before it fell out.

A hair in the head is worth two in the brush.

He used to have a crew cut, but the crew bailed out.

Skinheads come and go, but baldness is forever.

If I was a barber, there would be no hair.

He was a hair raiser in his youth.

To hell with nuclear fallout, I've got my own problems.

Bald heads cover highly developed brains.

Beauty

Beauty is when a face is an ornament rather than a means of identification.

Your packaging is great, people would never guess you've got nothing to sell.

Do you love me because I'm beautiful, or am I beautiful because you love me?

Anatomy is destiny.

Every woman in a tatty gown and old slippers dreams of being Cinderella.

Beauty is better than brains, because men see better than they think.

Time is a great healer, but a terrible beautician.

She has a beautiful face, unclouded by thought.

Some women are not really beautiful, they only look as though they are.

Your face is your passport to a better future.

Beauty is the index of a larger fact than wisdom.

Ugliness is superior to beauty because it lasts forever.

The more serious the face, the lovelier the smile.

Stupidity is acceptable, provided it's nicely packaged.

A good exterior is a silent recommendation.

Beautiful flowers sometimes have a foul scent.

Of course there is a distinction between the physically desirable and the ugly majority.

Beauty distorts perception.

Sure beauty is only skin deep, but what do you want, an adorable pancreas?

You notice a beauty, a charmer notices you.

So what if beauty is only skin deep, it's enough.

It's better to be beautiful than good, but better to be good than ugly.

Beauty may only be skin deep, but that's deep enough for most men.

Beauty charms a lover and terrifies a husband.

Beauty tempts others, poverty tempts beauty.

The best part of the banana is hidden from view.

I've never seen a smiling face that wasn't beautiful.

It's the beautiful birds that are caged.

Nothing is beautiful inside and outside.

To a pig, another pig is beautiful.

Beauty can afford to be kind, but seldom is.

If Jack is in love, he's no judge of Jill's beauty.

It's a phenomenon of nature that we don't have to communicate with it, to see it is enough.

Beauty is silent eloquence.

Beauty is a feast in itself.

Many women are not as beautiful as they are painted.

Beauty is proportionate to the amount of light and the depth of the bottle.

Beauty and chastity argue constantly.

She's not beautiful, she's merely aesthetically enhanced.

A beautiful typist may not be as efficient as an ugly one, but who cares?

Beauty is in the eye of the beholder.

Everything beautiful is loveable.

Before committing, visualise her without make-up.

Nature covers the ugliest souls with the most beautiful bodies.

Beauty must be shared, it should never be hoarded.

Fashion

If God had intended them to be lifted and separated, he would have put one on each shoulder.

Monkey see, monkey do.

Most fashion designers are men, whose greatest desire is to be a woman.

Isn't it clever how blondes dye their roots black?

Never in the history of fashion has so little covered so much that so badly needed to be covered up.

Her clothes are never out of style, they just look more ridiculous year after year.

Fashion can be bought, but style is inherent.

A fashion statement? No comment.

The latest thing in women's clothes is transvestites.

Her clothes are designed in Paris, but she wears them with an Australian accent.

Wearing sunglasses is optical seclusion.

Brevity is the soul of lingerie.

The latest fashions suit ten percent of the population, but ninety percent of people wear them.

She only wears designer clothes, but all her husbands are second hand.

If someone says an outfit suits you, they must think your other outfits don't.

She dresses at the top of her voice and the noise is deafening.

Every generation laughs at the old fashions, but pursues the new relentlessly.

No-one squeezes more into a bikini than she does.

Oh, I didn't recognise you with your clothes on.

She shows a lot of style, and the style shows a lot of woman.

You are ushered in according to your dress.

Fashions come and go, but style is eternal.

High heels were invented by a woman who was sick of being kissed on her forehead.

There she is, in an advanced state of nudity.

There's nothing tighter than next year's budget and last year's bikini.

That's an interesting outfit, do you think the style will ever come back into fashion?

Boy George is all England needs, another queen with no fashion sense.

A girdle holds a woman in when she goes out.

The love of fashion makes the economy go round.

It's not the cost of the strapless evening dress, it's the upkeep.

Nothing could ever replace the bikini, and nothing has.

The great thing about money is that it never clashes with anything you wear.

Her clothes are so tight that the men in the office can hardly breath.

Beneath this shabby exterior lies a total lack of character.

My dress is so low cut that I can hardly contain myself.

She went braless, and it was quite a let down.

Her neckline is near the waistline, low and behold.

Fashion is an induced epidemic.

There is nothing more fashionable than money.

Fashion makes women look better, and men look longer.

That's a lovely outfit you're almost wearing.

God sees the soul, man sees the clothes.

Weight

You don't have to be afraid to be seen with fat people, obesity isn't contagious.

Bulimia means you can have your cake and eat it too.

She's not thin, she's just too tall for her weight.

Obesity is a sign that something is eating you.

The cemeteries are full of skinny people.

Fat expands to fill that new dress that fitted perfectly a month ago.

A fat person is someone who exceeds the feed limit.

I watch my food, but I don't eat it.

The trouble with bucket seats in cars is that not everybody has the same size bucket.

Obesity is wide spread.

Diets are for those who are thick and tired of being fat.

I'm a fat anorexic.

Stand up and let two other people sit down.

I watch what I eat, and whatever I watch, I eat.

You can't be too rich or too thin.

How long does it take to get fat?

She goes to all the best restaurants, and one day she'll actually eat there.

Obesity is when you allow your appetite to punish you.

Anorexia is an optimistic stomach waiting for a pessimistic appetite.

The stomach is ungrateful. No matter what it had yesterday, it wants more today.

Obesity is a gain and a gain and a gain.

She's my two best friends.

Gluttony is not a secret vice.

Fat people are jolly because so much of them has a good time.

It isn't easy keeping your weight down and your spirits up.

You can trust a fat man, he'll never stoop to anything low.

The appetite grows by eating.

Open your mouth and say *moo.*

Obesity is a hand to mouth disease.

Even an Adam's apple would give her some shape.

Obesity is surplus gone to the waist.

The seafood diet: see food, eat it.

What doesn't go to waste goes to waist.

Outside every fat man there's a thin one who wants to get in.

To get thin, think thin.

If you don't steer clear, you spread.

Eat to live, not live to eat.

Obesity begins at home.

Inside every fat man there's a thin man wildly signalling to get out.

Diet is a four letter word.

The fatter the sow, the more she likes the mud.

How God must have laughed when he decided to make sprouts non-fattening.

A crash diet helps you lose weight fast and regain it gradually.

A fat person is too fat to fight and too slow to run away.

When dieting, if you show a loss, you've gained.

A glutton digs his own grave with his teeth.

A gourmet is a glutton with money.

The Arts

Art

This is either a terrible forgery or a brilliant original.

The hand can never create anything higher than the heart can inspire.

Art is not what the artist saw, but what his viewers see.

Art is a perceptual window through which each individual sees something different.

Art is whatever you can get the government to give you a grant for.

Art is passion and violence, not tepid elegance.

Art is composed of tears that are too deep to be expressed as sorrow.

Michelangelo saw an angel in the marble, and carved until he'd set it free.

Life imitates art more than art imitates life.

Art does not copy, it interprets.

To bleach ivory is to spoil nature by art.

Only an auctioneer can acclaim all schools of art equally.

It is a profound expression of mixed emotions.

Art is a collaboration between artist and God.

Art refers only to its own reality.

The purpose of art is to provide jobs for the security firms hired to protect it.

Art is a diamond with many facets.

Art is the exaggeration of an idea.

Art makes the divine visible.

Bad artists always admire each other's work.

Art is the ability to make something out of nothing, and sell it for something.

Art is the reasoned derangement of the senses.

Art happens.

Art reproduces imagination.

Art is the signature of civilisation.

Art is a revolt against man's fate.

Of all the lies, art is the least untrue.

Art is uncompromising, but life is full of compromises.

Pleasure is an infallible critical guide to art.

Art reproduces life with an enhanced meaning and in a more memorable form.

Art is long and life is short.

Art is an illusion, without which life would be a bore.

Art teaches nothing except the significance of life.

Out of chaos comes art.

It is a response to life that has to be created and cannot be copied.

Art does not take kindly to facts.

Art is man's striving toward immortality.

True art is rarely a verbatim translation.

Art takes reality by surprise, by condensing special moments into major emotion.

Art is I, science is we.

As time passes, the value of art increases, but it never improves.

Art disturbs, science reassures.

Art is the oldest enemy of ignorance.

Trendy art is a toy which belongs to a clique.

Art teaches us the significance of life.

Artists

An artist is the human debris that hangs around a work of art.

The more minimal the art, the greater the artist's explanation.

An artist's vision is limited to the cramped dimensions of his own ego.

An artist cannot explain his art any more than a plant can explain horticulture.

A good artist gives everything to his art, so that there's nothing left to give anyone else.

An artist is a dreamer, dreaming his own world.

An artist sings the song of the brush.

Artists either cater to the masses, or crawl to the elite.

Portraits reflect the artist as much as the sitter.

An artist bridges the chasm between his idea and the viewer's eye.

You cannot compare an artist's life with anything except an artist's life.

Nothing can come out of an artist that wasn't there already.

No sane man argues with an artist.

Rembrandt painted around seven hundred paintings, of which only three thousand still exist today.

Artists are by definition children.

An artist uses all his senses to depict the world as he perceives it.

When you see things as they really are, you cease to be an artist.

The end result of an artist's work depends more upon his mood than upon his subject.

An artist is his own fault.

Confidence in nonsense is a prerequisite for creativity.

Art must be articulate, but not the artist.

An artist dreams the actual world.

When we lose ourselves in art, we find ourselves.

Artists lie, but art never.

There are times when the artist should be hung instead of the painting.

An artist shuts his eyes in order to see.

We live in a rainbow of chaos.

I'd rather be a connoisseur than a painter.

Not to dare is to diminish.

The artistic temperament only affects amateurs.

An artist never finishes his work, he merely abandons it.

Bad artists always admire each other's work.

The painter's eye is to him what the lawyer's tongue is to him.

Craft can be taught, talent cannot.

Great artists are neither faithful husbands nor modest men.

An artist need only write well enough to sign contracts.

Look at what I produce, not at what I am.

Competitions are for athletes, not artists.

Every artist writes his own biography.

The true artist will let his family starve so that he can paint.

A bad architect's client plants vines.

I am not practising, I am working.

A professional artist is someone who is financially supported by another while he paints.

If he paints, he would rather write, and if he writes, he would rather paint.

An artist can produce from whatever materials are on hand.

Literature

Never judge a book by its movie.

Literature is an escape from your own life into someone else's.

Fiction has to make sense, so truth is naturally stranger.

Books are not lifeless bits of paper, they are minds that live on shelves.

This book has too much plot and not enough story.

I read part of it all the way through.

Read only a book that would impress others if you died in the middle of it.

This novel is not to be tossed aside lightly. Hurl it with great force.

If we assumed that anyone with a large vocabulary could write great literature, the dictionary should be the world's greatest literary masterpiece.

It doesn't matter how far fetched it is, great literature makes the reader willing to suspend disbelief.

In a book shop, temptation is irresistible.

Literature proclaims publicly what the writer hides from his immediate circle.

Smutty books show the world their own shame.

The person who doesn't read is no better than the one who can't read.

This book wasn't worth cutting a tree down for.

Literature lives on after its creator dies.

Some people wouldn't read even if books were banned.

A classic is a book everyone pretends to have read.

He writes for the reader who has put away comic books, but isn't yet ready for an editorial.

There are no fans, just customers.

Literature is about having sex, life is about having children.

Read it yourself and see why you shouldn't read it.

Some read to learn and some read to forget.

He mellowed before he ripened.

Literature is the lie that exposes the truth.

I never read a book before reviewing it; it prejudices me.

Literature is silent poetry spoken aloud.

A closed book is just a block of paper.

The books I haven't begun are better than the books others have finished.

The covers of some books are too far apart.

No-one ever returns books. I should know, I have a library full of borrowed books.

Americans like fat books and thin women.

We are what we read.

Instinct and talent are not enough.

Literature lives on after its author dies.

Literary men are a perpetual priesthood.

The road to ignorance is paved with good editions.

If a fool peers in, a wise man won't peer out.

Literature is half business and half craft.

Milton wrote Paradise Lost. When his wife died, he wrote Paradise Regained.

The most important aspect of any book is the reader's interpretation of it.

We are not content with imagination or reality, we want conclusion.

Books had instant replay long before television did.

Music

Music is what feelings sound like.

Music is thought with the heart and felt with the brain.

Classical music was written by famous dead foreigners.

God must love pianists, he made so many of them.

Music is the universal language of mankind.

Rock and roll is music heard through the feet and not the ears.

Music is the speech of angels.

Composers can see music.

There should be music in each and every single home, except next door.

Jazz is an appeal to the emotions by an attack on the nerves.

Hell is full of amateur violinists.

Van Gogh wouldn't have done it if there had been stereo.

AM stands for Absolute Moron, but I'm too polite to say what FM stands for.

The grandeur of man lies in song, not in thought.

An oboe is an ill woodwind that nobody blows good.

The sweetest songs tell the saddest thoughts.

Music is perpetual, hearing it is intermittent.

Opera is full of dying heroes who burst into song.

It is your duty to drown bad music in conversation.

Music plucks at the heartstrings.

Music comes closer than anything else to expressing the inexpressible.

If the music is good, people talk, and if the music is bad, people listen.

Music expresses that which cannot be said, but on which it is impossible to remain silent.

The first thing a child learns when he gets a drum is that he will never get another one.

How wonderful opera would be if it had no singers.

When you separate speech from art, the result is music.

Music is food for the ears.

Never buy a Stradivarius, you can't get spare parts for them.

The song has ended, but the melody lingers on.

Music is poetry that speaks to each person individually.

From the enlightenment of music comes the wisdom of silence.

Old musicians never die, they just decompose.

From the persistence of noise comes the insistence of rage.

Music is a celebration of life.

Who hears music feels his solitude peopled at once.

Music doesn't remember those who tamper with it.

The trouble with country music is that it travels to the city.

Musicians blow their own horns.

Vincent van Gogh had no ear for music.

If music be the food of love, there must be many people with indigestion.

Musicians paint their pictures on silence.

Of all the noises, music is the most agreeable.

If it wasn't for music, some dances would be considered obscene.

Beethoven was so deaf he thought he was a painter.

Plagiarism

That which we think is original is based on the gist of what we no longer specifically remember.

The worst copy the best.

We disfigure someone else's thoughts to disguise them as our own.

How am I supposed to invent ideas that no-one's ever expressed before?

Any fool can reproduce another fool's work.

Originality is better only because it provides the basis for the improvement.

It's not easy finding showing the way to a route you haven't taken.

The wages of sin are royalties.

Imitation is the sincerest form of plagiarism.

I am but a gatherer and a disposer of other men's stuff.

Originality is the art of concealing your source.

It's not so much that I'm honest, it's just that I don't have much scope to steal.

Even our thoughts are based on other people's thinking.

An ant which imitates an elephant is likely to be trod on.

Most of the human race goes through life without ever having an original thought.

They say it's better to fail in originality, than to succeed in imitation. They lie.

Stealing from the moderns is plagiarism, stealing from the ancients is erudition.

Creativity is great, but plagiarism is faster.

Pickpockets always keep their hands in their own pockets when they're not working.

The best way to have a good idea is to read someone else's good ideas.

More than half of what is perceived to be original is imitation.

You can only practice plagiarism successfully if you're already famous.

Some ideas grow better when transplanted.

Of course I steal, but only from the best writers.

Nothing is new except the way it's arranged.

Fine words, I wonder where he stole them?

Utter originality is a myth.

If I copy another's beauty, I am innocent. I am only guilty if I copy his faults.

Plagiarists feed their lean thoughts on the fat of someone else's ideas.

If you discarded what you owe to others, there would be nothing left.

Those who steal to appear intelligent to fools, appear foolish to the intelligent.

To steal from one is plagiarism. To steal from many is research.

I steal from others, and blend them into my own.

To think is not enough, you must have an idea.

Adam was the world's only non-plagiarist.

Originality is undetected plagiarism.

When young, we imitate others. When old, we imitate ourselves.

No man has yet become great by imitation.

It's easier to merge than to invent.

We imitate those whom we least resemble.

Imitation is the sincerest form of flattery.

It's immoral, but if you must do it, use only the best sources.

Only a mean thief and a successful author plunder the dead.

Immature artists imitate, mature artists steal.

When a frog tries to puff itself up as big as an elephant, it bursts.

Writers

No tears in the writer, no tears in the reader.

A professional writer is an amateur who didn't quit.

Freelance writers have the freedom to starve anywhere.

Writing keeps us from believing everything we read.

How do you know what you think until you see what you say?

It's as easy to think a book as it is hard to actually write it.

Words are the thread on which we string our experiences.

Your manuscript is both good and original, but the part that is good is not original, and the part that is original is not good.

If I only had six months to live, I'd type faster.

A manuscript is something submitted in haste and returned at leisure.

Madness prompts, and reason writes.

Some people contain a single book, others contain a library.

Writing is an honourable profession because doctors earn by disease, priests by sin and lawyers by argument.

So tell me, how did you love my book?

I love writing, it's the paperwork I hate.

The most essential gift for a writer is a built-in bullshit detector.

I'm a writer. What a coincidence, I'm a reader.

I love the swirl and swing of words as they tangle with human emotion.

If you want to make me cry, you have to feel grief yourself.

The last infirmity of a mundane mind is to write a book.

Every great man has disciples, but it's always Judas who writes the biography.

It took me fifteen years to discover that I couldn't write, but I couldn't give it up because I'd become too famous.

If you have any comments, write them on the back of a cheque.

Poetry is pain washed in tears.

This morning I took out a comma, and this afternoon I put it back.

If you want to be a reader, read. But if you want to be a writer, write.

Words are hooks from which ideas hang.

I'm a bad writer, but so many people have bad taste.

There are three essential rules for writing a novel, but nobody knows what they are.

It took me years to finish my first novel, because I'm such a slow reader.

An autobiography is a record of the good you intended to do, minus the bad you did.

Keep a diary and one day it will keep you.

A novelist lives off his imagination.

The pen is the tongue of the head, a silent utterer of words for the eye.

The ratio of literacy to illiteracy is constant, but nowadays the illiterates can write.

Easy reading is hard writing.

No author is a genius to his publisher.

Satire is moral outrage disguised as comic art.

Some people don't write, they type.

From the first page I was convulsed with laughter, one day I'll read it further.

Writers are too self centred to be lonely.

He is a writer for the ages, of between four and eight.

Literature is news that stays news.

Attitude

Attitude

You get what you settle for.

Everything looks yellow to a jaundiced eye.

He who has confidence designs his own road.

You can complain because roses have thorns, or rejoice because thorns have roses.

I wish I was what I used to be, when I wanted to be what I am now.

Attitude decides whether you'll grow up to be Cinderella or the cruel stepsister.

Don't be so narrow minded that your ears touch each other.

Don't be so broadminded that your brains fall out.

A duck looks calm on the surface, but it is paddling like hell below.

You only strive if you believe you have a greater possibility.

A timid question always elicits a confident answer.

When you've got the charisma, you don't need the nudity.

We see things not as they are, but as we are.

The new broom sweeps cleaner only because of its novelty to the sweeper.

The Wright brothers flew through the smoke screen of impossibility.

The mystery of life is in the eye of the beholder.

If you can conceive the plan, you can achieve the reality.

Grab the opportunity now so that you don't have to regret what might have been.

We are all half moon, half sun.

If you look at life in a particular way, there is always cause for alarm.

If you didn't close your eyes sometimes, ultimately there would be nothing worth looking at.

Nature hates monopolies and exceptions.

A wise man's question contains half the answer.

When you do what you can, you become what you do.

We lop away superfluous branches so that bearing boughs may live.

Everyone follows a confident man.

If you can't find peace within, you won't find it elsewhere.

Between a rock and a hard place.

Don't compromise yourself, you're all you've got.

If you think you're a third rate citizen, you are.

Don't bite the hand that has your allowance in it.

Nothing is more stilted than the effort to seem natural.

To find the limits of the possible, go beyond them.

If you keep an open mind, people throw rubbish into it.

He who has no fire in himself cannot warm others.

If you can't be loyal to your own principles, you can't be loyal to anything.

Don't look back, someone's gaining on you.

A smile is one curve that can set a lot of things straight.

We can't all, and some just won't.

Attitude is all that separates excellence from mediocrity.

I can't decide whether indecision is a good or bad quality.

They conquer who believe they can.

Boredom

I wish I'd known you while you were still alive.

You are the champion of monotony.

I could wade through your deepest thoughts without getting my ankles wet.

A bore deprives you of solitude without providing you with company.

A bore has a good mind to give you a good listening to.

I spent a year in that town one weekend.

If you ask a bore the time, he launches into the history of the clock.

I don't mind telling you my story twice, but why should I have to listen to yours twice?

The cure for boredom is curiosity.

We can forgive those who bore us easier than we can forgive those that find us boring.

A variety of nothing is inferior to a monopoly of something.

A bore has never had an unexpressed thought in his entire life.

You are a triumph of the embalmer's art.

The secret of being a successful bore is to tell everyone everything.

I'm so successful now that when I bore someone, they think the fault is theirs.

A bore consumes twice his weight a year in other people's patience.

He is a man of few words, but the problem is he keeps repeating them.

I don't want to bore you, but since there's no-one else around, you'll have to do.

Boredom is to be slain by the jawbone of an ass.

An educated bore is able to be boring on a much greater variety of subjects.

It's not so much that he won't stop talking, it's that he won't let you stop listening.

Boredom is a sign of intelligence.

A bore is someone who can change the subject back to his topic faster than you can change it back to yours.

Died at thirty, buried at sixty.

You are not only a bore yourself, but you cause boredom in others.

A bore is someone who talks in other people's sleep.

Familiarity breeds contempt and takes the edge off admiration.

A day away from him is like a month in the country.

Everybody is somebody's bore.

Anticipation of tomorrow is no consolation for today.

So boring he couldn't even entertain a doubt.

It's only interesting if you're interested.

A dull man is always sure, a sure man is always dull.

He's only dull until you get to know him, and after that he's just plain boring.

A bore is a person who's had a charisma bypass.

His shortcoming is his long staying.

He has a flood of words and a drought of ideas.

A bore keeps talking long after you've stopped listening.

Early to bed and early to rise makes a man boring.

A bore falls asleep in the middle of a nap.

People to whom nothing exciting ever happens, cannot understand the importance of events.

Every hero becomes a bore eventually.

A bore reminds you of the tedium of life.

Conceit

Me and my elephant, said the flea.

There are times when I think I'll die of an overdose of satisfaction.

There, but for the grace of God, goes God.

He thinks he's better than everyone else, when everyone knows I'm the best.

There's something to be said for conceit, so let's say it.

Today an ostrich feather, tomorrow a blue boa.

The bigger his head is, the easier it is to fill his shoes.

It's not conceited to admire anyone that talented, who just happens to be me.

What a rotten opinion I have of myself, and how little I deserve it.

Conceit is obesity of the brain.

A conceited person is someone of low intelligence, who is more interested in himself than in me.

Admiration is the polite recognition of another's resemblance to ourselves.

I'm not conceited, although I have every right to be.

Conceit is the anaesthetic that dulls the pain of stupidity.

Admiring your own halo causes a pain in the neck.

He thinks people who say *Oh God* when they see him, are religious.

No matter what others think of him, he fascinates himself.

Each morning I awake to the supreme pleasure of being me.

The love of oneself is the beginning of a lifelong romance.

I'm always right when other people are wrong.

Conceit is a hat covering an empty head.

If ever anyone loved him as much as he loves himself, it would be the world's greatest romance.

An egotist talks about himself instead of talking about you.

He sings his own praises, but it's an unaccompanied solo.

She never takes hot showers, they cloud the mirror.

When he fails, it's God's fault, but his successes are his own achievement.

Success has turned his head and left it facing in the wrong direction.

He never says a bad word about anyone, but that's because he only talks about himself.

It doesn't matter where he goes, as long as he's in the driver's seat.

Blowing your own horn sends your battery flat.

Better a self confessed sinner than a conceited saint.

If you pat yourself on the back too hard, you fall flat on your face.

The whistle isn't what makes the train go.

Conceit is God's gift to insignificant people.

The head swells when the mind stops expanding.

When success goes to the head, it comes out of the mouth.

The bigger a man's head, the worse his headache.

All the best poets are dead, and I'm not feeling too well myself.

A nightingale sings with its eyes shut, conscious only of the beauty of its own voice.

When God invented man, he wanted them all to look like me.

If I hadn't been born me, that's who I would have liked to be.

I'm not conceited, I'm perfect.

The rooster thinks the sun rises early to hear him crow.

Cynicism

Religion is man's attempt to communicate with the weather.

A cynic sees murder as a sign of civilisation.

All the best things in life are already taken.

When a cynic smells flowers, he looks for a coffin.

A cynic is someone who is prematurely disappointed in the future.

He can't wait for the future so that he can look back with regret.

The person who has no problems doesn't understand life.

When everything is going great, you've overlooked something.

The reverse side has its own reverse side.

If things don't improve soon, you'll have to stop cheering me up.

It is difficult to overcome my desires, and impossible to satisfy them.

Under that happy face, you're just as miserable as me.

If everything is going my way, I must be headed in the wrong direction.

A cynic begins as an actor in a comedy and ends as a spectator to a tragedy.

A pedestrian is a motorist who thought the fuel gauge worked.

How long can the meek hang onto the earth once they inherit it?

Putting on a coat doesn't make it any warmer outside.

I'm not cynical, I just have an incredible lack of awe for everything and everyone.

A cynic is just tired of being so damn happy.

Cynicism is a trip through a sewer in a glass bottomed boat.

Love is what happens to two people before they know each other well.

I don't care who you are, Fatso, get your reindeer off my roof.

A cynic is not a vegetarian because he loves animals, but because he hates plants.

A cynic sees life as it is, not as it's supposed to be.

A cynic absorbs sunshine and laughter, but radiates doom and gloom.

There is something ridiculous about those we have ceased to love.

Gardening is not so much about growing flowers as it is about burying seeds.

A cynic is a well balanced individual with a chip on each shoulder.

Quality is just an excuse for lack of quantity.

A cynic laughs at everything, provided it isn't amusing.

Our lives are greedy pilgrimages in search of hungry recipients.

A cynic is a disillusioned idealist.

If love is the answer, please rephrase the question.

He's full of the joy of almost living.

Cynics are never disappointed in anyone because they expected the worst anyway.

A cynic searches for an honest man with a stolen torch.

A cynic complains about the noise when opportunity knocks.

He reads the obituary notices to cheer himself up.

Every day is painful, and on your very last day, you die.

A man wants to be a woman's first love, and a woman wants to be a man's last love.

A cynic is a philosopher with fangs.

When the heart fills up, the brain empties.

Tears will get you sympathy, sweat will get you results.

A cynic knows there's no limit to how bad things can get.

A smile is just a frown upside down.

A cynic is someone who knows the price of everything and the value of nothing.

Hope

Extreme hope is born of extreme misery.

When you reach the end of your tether, hope is what keeps you hanging on.

Hope's road provides the most agreeable route.

Please calm down, I'm hysterical enough for all of us.

We hope vaguely, but dread precisely.

If it wasn't for hope, the heart would break.

We would not work if we did not hope to benefit from it.

Hope is a minor form of despair, disguised as a virtue.

If you have abandoned hope, you have welcomed desperation.

We call doubt hope, to dispel the fear of the truth.

When hope alters its shape, it takes on the form of despair.

You can leave a log in the river for ten years, and it still won't be a crocodile.

He who lives on hope dances to a terrible tune.

Hope is the front we put on when we don't want to face the truth.

Hope is the anchor of the soul.

Nothing inspires hope like the first few days of a new diet.

A reasonable probability is the only certainty, so dream on.

Hope is faith holding its hand out to comfort you.

If you do not hope, you will never know what lies beyond your hopes.

Never deprive anyone of hope, it may be all they have.

Hope temporarily uplifts the heart weighted down with sorrow.

Hope is socially acceptable optimism.

An optimist is a hope addict.

There is an island of hope in the ocean of difficulty.

Hope is a bad guide, but a good travelling companion.

Hope is the silent voice that tells us tomorrow will be better.

It's hard to hope with a hangover.

God grant me wondrous things, but let me strive for what I can attain myself.

Hope is the dream of the waking man.

Unreasonable hope is the wish for a happy outcome, not the result of good judgement.

Too low they build who build beneath the stars.

You cannot hope for it once you have seen it.

You can cast your bread upon the waters, but don't expect it to come back toasted and buttered.

Hope is the hidden ingredient in any doctor's prescription.

There is no winter in the land of hope.

If you live on hope, you will die of hunger.

Something will turn up.

Hope is a risk that must be taken.

What is past hope is ready for grief.

Hope is the cloak covering truth's nakedness.

A hundred men with a hundred dreams, one of which may come true.

Hope is a by-product of fear.

He fishes on who catches one.

If it does you good, hope on.

Wishing is to want something for nothing.

Optimism

Cheer up, things are getting worse at a slower rate.

If you're going after Moby Dick, take the tartar sauce.

The less you have, the more you have to look forward to.

We are completely outnumbered and surrounded, they can't possibly escape.

An optimist is someone who's always cheerful about someone else's problems.

It takes optimism to get out of bed in the morning.

An optimist sees the doughnut, a pessimist sees the hole in the middle.

Murphy was an optimist.

An optimist is an octogenarian who marries a young bride and buys a house near a school.

This is the best day I've ever had, but I'm sure tomorrow will be better.

Grey skies are just clouds.

A fifty year old optimist knows nothing about life.

You don't get eyestrain from looking at the bright side of life.

When you've sunk to rock bottom, the only way out is up.

The optimist believes he has the best of everything, and the pessimist fears he might be right.

In my darkest hour, I can see the moon and stars.

You're as happy as you decide you want to be.

It's always easy the night before to get up early the next morning.

I'm an optimist, but I still take an umbrella if it looks like rain.

An optimist is the best man at his friend's wedding.

In the midst of winter, I discovered I had within me an invincible summer.

When you look for the good in everything, you find it.

An optimist makes the best of a bad situation.

Optimism is the delusion that everything ugly is beautiful.

An optimist is someone who actually enjoys the scenery on a detour.

An optimist expects his dreams to come true.

Somewhere in the world, this dark night is already over.

An optimist buys a brush with that bottle of hair restorer.

When the sun disappears, the stars come out.

Optimism is the delusion that life is great even when those around you are suicidal.

A flat tyre is only flat at the bottom.

Optimism is a passport to a better future.

An optimist looks for a pearl, a pessimist fears salmonella.

An optimist does the cryptic crossword with a pen.

Give me a long enough lever, and I will move the earth.

The optimist's glass is half full, the pessimist's is half empty.

All optimists over fifty are alive and well and living in institutions.

An optimist is a neurotic pessimist who is determined to be cheerful.

An optimist is wrong as often as the pessimist, but he's much happier.

An optimist doesn't believe the end of the world will be as bad as everyone thinks it will be.

An optimist happily considers how unhappy he would be if he wasn't optimistic.

An optimist makes the best of a bad situation.

Optimism is the digitalis of failure.

Pessimism

Life is unsure. Eat your dessert first.

The light at the end of the tunnel is an oncoming train.

In the event of an accident, I'm not surprised.

A pessimist is someone who feels bad when he feels good, for fear of feeling worse when he feels better.

Cheer up, things could get worse. So I cheered up and they got worse.

Chicken Little only has to be right once.

When you come to the end of a perfect day, remember it's not over yet.

Everything is somewhere else, and you need transport to get there.

He not only expects the worst, he makes the worst of whatever happens.

A happy man is someone who hasn't heard the news yet.

It's lonely in the saddle when your horse is dead.

For every positive action, there is an equal and opposite negative reaction.

A shin is a device for finding sharp edges in the dark.

A pessimist thinks everyone is as nasty as himself, and he hates them for it.

Bad is never good until worse happens.

A pessimist isn't afraid to show his terror.

A pessimist thinks the whole world is against him, and he's right.

I'm not a pessimist, just a disillusioned optimist.

A pessimist sees only the thorns on roses, but an optimist sees only the roses amongst the thorns.

Pessimism is a triumph of worry over matter.

We change not because we see the light, but because we feel the heat.

Pessimism arises from the impotence to act upon certain knowledge effectively.

After things go from bad to worse, the cycle repeats itself.

If it's handed to him on a silver platter, he'll wait for it to tarnish.

A pessimist designed air bags and seat belts.

A pessimist knows his worst nightmares will come true.

It only takes a single cloud to eclipse the sun.

A pessimist isn't sure the tide will ever come in again.

Failure has gone to his head.

The hardness of the butter is proportionate to the softness of the bread.

Every silver lining has a cloud.

He burns his bridges before he gets to them.

You have to have the courage of your own pessimism.

If germ warfare doesn't get us, the atom bomb will.

When you're up to your armpits in alligators, it's hard to remember that your original intention was to drain the swamp.

He hopes for nothing good but fears everything bad.

As soon as you get your head above water, someone steals your flippers.

If it wasn't for the optimist, the pessimist would never know how happy he was.

A pessimist can't get going, an optimist can't stop.

Opportunity always knocks at the least opportune moment.

A pessimist is someone who lives with an optimist.

A pessimist is never disappointed.

This is a man who has nothing to eat but food.

Business

Advertising

What the big print giveth, the fine print taketh away.

Stock up now and save. Limit one per customer.

If you didn't ignore me, I wouldn't have to exaggerate so much.

Half of what is spent on advertising is wasted, but which half?

Advertising invents a cure for which there is no disease.

Advertising is proof that famous people will endorse anything for money.

If it looks complicated, they lose interest.

Advertising promises more than the product can possibly deliver.

Advertising raises the standard of longing.

A viewer who fast forwards the ads is the moral equivalent of a thief.

It's what it's not that makes it what it is.

Nothing reveals a nation as clearly as the majority of it's advertisements.

A sponsor is the golden goose for whom others lay the egg.

Advertising is telling lies that attract shoplifters.

Advertising is what puts the wonder into Wonder Bread.

Advertising is the mother of desire.

Advertisers incite others to pursue pleasure, but they ignore it themselves.

Advertising is when you reward your appetite for punishing you.

None of us likes the smell, but we all know what the skunk is famous for.

Advertising convinces teenagers they would be social outcasts if their designer labels weren't visible.

Advertising makes people obsessive about owning something they didn't know existed the day before.

People keep advertising for lost animals, when everyone knows animals can't read.

Advertising gives the public credit for too much intelligence.

A good thing sells itself, a bad thing advertises itself.

Advertising is aimed at the person you would like to be.

Advertising gives us a choice of what we have a choice of.

Advertising is the science of getting people to suspend intelligence long enough to get money from them.

Of course you can blame the manufacturer, he has to approve the advertisement.

If I can't flatter you into buying it, perhaps I can scare you into it.

Advertising creates the need that manufacturers fill.

Propaganda is political advertising.

Dog for sale: eats anything, fond of children.

Advertising is eighty percent confusion and fifteen percent commission.

Nothing exceeds the vanity of our existence like the folly of our pursuits.

One advertisement is worth a dozen editorials.

If we spent half as much on improving it as we spent on promoting it, the product would sell itself.

It gets late early out here.

If you don't put petrol in, the car won't go anywhere.

Why do they advertise *free gifts*, when gifts are free anyway?

If you don't beat the bush, someone else will catch the bird.

Banking

But I can't be overdrawn, I've still got twenty cheques left.

Banks don't have principles, but they believe in interest.

When a bank lends you money, you are everlastingly indebted.

If you owe the bank a hundred dollars, that's your problem. If you owe the bank a hundred million dollars, that's the bank's problem.

Bankers are the same as anyone else, only richer.

If I'm such a poor risk, how come I owe them so much?

A banker is a shark that attacks little fish who swim out of their financial depths.

A bank is where you keep your money until the government asks you to send it.

Borrowing money from a bank is like throwing meatballs at a hungry dog.

Where are the fool and his money when you need a loan?

A bank gives you an umbrella when the sun is shining, and takes it back when it starts to rain.

Banking is the ability to do business with other people's money.

The shortest queue always moves the slowest.

So many cheques, so little money.

Bankers are predators who prey on the poor to finance the ventures of the wealthy.

When he borrows money, it's against his principle to pay interest, and against his interest to pay the principal.

We have an agreement with the bank, they do not sell groceries, and we do not cash cheques.

For every cent they lend you, they want a dollar back.

Of course money grows on trees, the problem is that the banks own the branches.

This is a great country, where else could I earn enough to pay the interest on what I owe?

Banks exaggerate what you owe them.

They were friendly enough when you borrowed the money, but when they want it back, they don't care whether or not they make an enemy of you in the process.

Rob the bank before it robs you.

A banker is an optimistic pawnbroker, hoping you'll default.

Banking is a career from which no-one ever really recovers.

If your bank manager agrees with you, he needs you more than you need him.

Every time I need money, I suffer from withdrawal symptoms.

If you think no-one cares, try skipping a mortgage payment.

Bankers buy and sell, and live on the loss.

When you've got them by their mortgages, their hearts and minds will follow.

Parents are bankers provided by nature.

A banker is a nasty little miser who spends all day counting other people's money.

When Nick Leeson wrote a cheque, the bank bounced.

The flaws in the criminal's character are the bank manager's special talents.

What you don't owe, won't hurt you.

Borrowing money from a bank is like competing in a bleeding competition against the blood bank.

A banker will never go to hell, because he has no soul.

If you can afford the interest, you don't need the loan.

Put your money in trust, but don't put your trust in money.

Business

Greed is good.

It's a rat race, and you constantly have to keep an eye on the cat.

A holding company is where you keep your money until the auditors stop looking for it.

If you think it's confusing now, wait until you really understand it.

A verbal contract isn't worth the paper it's written on.

Why go somewhere else and be cheated when you can come here?

If it works well, they stop making it.

Light gains make heavy purses.

He who wishes to be rich in a day will be bankrupt in a year.

Trust only those who have as much to lose as you do.

You buy, therefore I'm rich.

An auctioneer announces with a hammer that he's picked a pocket with his tongue.

The beginning is the most important part.

The safest way to double your money is to fold it in two and put it away.

Capital is past savings accumulated for future production.

When a project doesn't work, look for the part you thought was least important.

Keep your head down and your profits go up.

Anyone can carve a career for himself using someone else's chisel.

Cheat me on price, but not on what I purchase.

A crook is a business rival who has just left the room.

If the profits are great, the risks are great.

Quality is proportionate to commitment, regardless of the field chosen.

Salesmen are optimists, accountants are pessimists.

What can I do you for?

Bulls and bears have never caused as many stock losses as bum steers.

Disorder defeats itself.

Profit is the overpricing you can extract from the public without resorting to violence.

Fools rush in where wise men fear to trade.

How come there is only one Monopolies Commission?

If you can't hide it, make it a feature.

Live together like brothers, but do business like strangers.

You can dine a man out of his principles.

Be nice to everyone on your way up, because you might pass them again on your way down.

Insider trading is when you steal too fast.

Farming is easy when you plough with a pencil.

Never negotiate before ten am or after four pm. Before ten, you seem anxious and after four, desperate.

Count your blessings while your opposition is adding up their troubles.

Business is never lost. If you didn't get it, your competitor did.

Sprinkle sewage over food and it all becomes sewage.

Transactions speak louder than words.

A clean desk is the sign of a cluttered drawer.

Industry breaks the chains of poverty.

A man who cannot smile all day should never open a shop.

No matter who rules, the merchant reigns.

Committees

If Moses had set up a committee, the Jews would still be in Egypt.

A committee is made up of a group of people who spend hours keeping minutes.

A committee is a group of people who collectively suffer from analysis paralysis.

A camel is what a horse would look like if it was designed by a committee.

Progress might have been all right once, but it went on too long.

Don't try to stem the tide, move the beach.

If it doesn't work, expand it.

Include me out.

A committee consists of five people: one does the work, three criticise him, and one reports back to the boss.

After the problem has been resolved, the committee is never dissolved.

A committee is a cul de sac down which ideas are lured and quietly strangled.

It isn't that they can't find a solution, it's that they don't understand the problem.

It takes a long time to find a shorter way.

Greatness isn't built on agreement, but on the death of those who oppose you.

The best way to slow down progress is to form a committee to speed it up.

You know you're successful if the meeting doesn't start until you arrive.

When in doubt, committee.

All those opposed, raise your hand and say, *I resign*.

Two negatives make an affirmative.

Inside every small problem there is a larger one waiting to get out.

If the last two people on earth were politicians, they would form a committee.

People in groups agree to action which, individually, they know is stupid.

Committees are so important that sub-committees have to be appointed to do the work.

Three people, four opinions.

When all is said and nothing is done, the meeting is adjourned.

The most successful committee consists of three people, two of whom are absent.

The minimum criteria required becomes the maximum value adopted.

The person most opposed to serving on the committee is always appointed the chairman.

Their expenditure of words is always greater than the outcome of the income.

Only those who agree with us have any intelligence.

Never hold discussions with the monkey if the organ grinder is present.

Their solutions cause problems.

Those who learn nothing from past meetings are condemned to repeat them again and again.

The approach to the problem is more important than its solution.

A group of the unwilling, selected from the unqualified, doing the unnecessary.

If there's a worse way to do it, the committee will find it.

When committees are formed to solve a problem, the committee sooner or later becomes more important than the original problem.

Nothing is impossible for those who don't have to do it themselves.

The Holy Trinity is a committee of god.

The purpose of a committee is to homogenise thinking.

Committees meet to decide when the next meeting should be postponed to.

You can't out-talk a man who doesn't know what he's talking about.

The solution of one problem leads to the creation of dozens of others.

Employment

If you pay peanuts, you get monkeys.

Those who think it can't be done shouldn't interrupt those doing it.

If you make an ass of yourself, people will ride you.

This is merely a suggestion, you don't have to do it if you don't mind being unemployed.

The reward for a job well done is another job.

Maybe hard work never killed anyone, but why take a chance?

We're overpaying him, but he's worth it.

Never underestimate the power of the dork side of the force.

Work expands to fill the time allotted for its completion.

If you worry about your job, you will be rewarded with ulcers.

The purpose of a holiday is to let employees know they're not indispensable.

Employment is a dreadful affliction suffered by those who want to go fishing.

If you can do a half assed job of anything, you're the one eyed man in the kingdom of the blind.

Hire a teenager, they know it all.

Productivity is in the eye of the beholder.

There is no job so simple that someone can't stuff it up.

Nothing improves a joke as much as telling it to employees.

If a cluttered desk indicates a cluttered mind, what does an empty desk signify?

Seminars demonstrate who the company can do without.

Monday is the root of all evil.

You can rest all you like when you're dead.

If the coffee breaks get any longer, they'll be late getting home.

The boss is the idiot who keeps interrupting to ask you to do something else.

Work is the greatest asset in the world, and should be preserved for future generations.

When the tree is full, only the choicest fruit is selected.

The best blessing is when the work you do is the hobby you love.

You have to speak up to be heard, but sometimes you have to shut up to be appreciated.

Beware of all enterprises that require new clothes.

Every job is easy for the person who doesn't have to do it.

I owe, I owe, it's off to work I go.

Nothing is as permanent as what began as a temporary arrangement.

Executives hold expensive conventions at the best resorts, to find ways to cut costs.

Everyone loads a willing horse.

When he left, there was no vacancy to fill.

Don't think of me as your boss, I'm merely a workmate who's never wrong.

Do someone a favour, and before you know it, it's your job.

He stopped looking for work the minute he found a job.

Better to be a third class executive than a first class janitor.

Nepotism is relative.

The boss delegates authority, shifts blame and takes credit.

I like well informed workers, as long as their views coincide with mine.

A secretary is someone who gets paid to type while she looks for a husband.

By the time the boss gets back from his holiday, everyone in the office feels rested.

A born executive is the boss's son.

Expertise

Everyone loves goodness, but no-one wants to live with the saint.

The further the expert has travelled, the greater his expertise.

If you focus your attention on the tricks of the trade, you don't learn the trade.

A cobbler makes good shoes because he makes nothing else.

An expert: an ex is a has-been and a spurt is a drip under pressure.

It's not that he's right more often than other people, but he's wrong for more sophisticated reasons.

An expert is someone who gets paid to show other people how to work.

A consultant knows a hundred ways of making love, but remains a virgin.

Consistency requires me to be as ignorant today as I was a year ago.

The difficult is done at once, the impossible takes a little longer.

Everyone practices the skill he knows best.

Because I've already made all the mistakes, I know how to avoid making them again.

Expertise has raised our ignorance to a higher level.

I pay the teacher, but the other children educate my child.

Expertise is a matter of persisting after everyone else gave up.

An efficiency expert saves money by cutting down on other people's expenses.

An expert doesn't know the answers either, but he gets paid more to look for them.

In an amateur's mind there are many possibilities, in an expert's mind there are only a few.

Those who are slow to learn assume speed represents a lack of knowledge.

The foolish ask questions the wise cannot answer.

Convents hate a saint in their midst.

Just because experts agree, it doesn't mean they're right.

The trouble with experts is that they think in grooves.

Experts are always imported from the overseas head office to do what the locals are too incompetent to do on their own.

A stupid comment sounds better in French, but it's still a stupid comment.

He not only overflowed with knowledge, but he frolicked in the sewerage.

You can't manage too many pumpkins in water, one pops up while you're trying to hold another down.

He that knows little, repeats it often.

A consultant confirms advice on a course already decided on.

Experts are like statistics, they testify for whoever pays the highest wage.

If the world blew up, an expert would be there saying it couldn't be done.

An expert is an ordinary person, away from home, who gives advice.

A great deal can be crammed into an empty head.

If you consult enough experts, you can confirm any opinion.

An expert spends his time analysing why yesterday's predictions didn't materialise today and won't be realised tomorrow.

If I had read as much as other men, I still would not know more than them.

An expert has stopped guessing, he knows for sure.

The expert's skill is the buyer's security.

He refuses bribes, but puts his hand out anyway.

An expert is a little squirt who thinks he's a fountain of wisdom.

The self-proclaimed expert is also self appointed.

Statistics

Although traffic accidents increase annually there have been fewer fatalities, and scientists now conclude that pedestrians are getting stronger.

There is reliable data to prove that wedding cake diminishes sexual desire.

The main function of statistics is to support statisticians.

A statistician is someone who's really good with figures, but doesn't have sufficient personality to become an accountant.

Always double check the calculations that support a calculated risk.

If crime keeps dropping at the current rate, the police force should be obsolete within two years.

One person's constant is another person's variable.

A statistician draws a precise conclusion from an unwarranted assumption to a foregone conclusion.

The less conclusive the result, the more elaborate the graph.

Every two minutes another statistic is created.

The word *statistics* was formulated from the Latin, meaning *to baffle them with bullshit.*

If forty percent of road fatalities are caused by drink drivers, then non-drinkers are more dangerous on the roads because they cause sixty percent of accidents.

Every second of every day, somewhere in the world, a woman gives birth. She must be found and stopped immediately.

Half the people in the world are below average.

Statistics show that one in three people suffer from mental illness. That means that if your two best friends are okay, you're nuts.

Everything has a fifty percent probability, but the odds are ninety percent against you.

A single death is a tragedy. A million deaths is a statistic.

Statistics reveal that if we continued to use our old detergents and lived with the stains, we would have thirty percent fewer commercials.

Your statistics make no noise in my frying pan.

If you can't convince them, confuse them.

Longevity has at last been conclusively proven to be the result of being born so long ago.

The latest figures released reveal that cigarettes and car accidents are the main cause of statistics.

Old statisticians never die, they just average out.

Liars figure figures don't lie.

All generalisations are false, including this one.

Only ten percent of the best are in the top ten percent.

Ninety eight percent of smokers die before the age of a hundred years.

Like a bikini, what they reveal is suggestive, but what they conceal is vital.

There are three kinds of lies: lies, damn lies, and statistics.

Statistics confirm that since capital punishment was reintroduced, none of those executed have re-offended.

Ten percent of men like women with fat legs, thirty percent like women with thin legs, and the remaining sixty percent prefer something in between.

The latest figures reveal that, as a result of overwork, executives are dying like flies on golf courses.

Twenty percent of all accidents in Sweden involve a moose.

Unions

If your employer gets up your nose, picket.

If it wasn't for demonstrations, they wouldn't have a social life.

It's not a matter of freedom, it's a question of who you're chained to.

I'll give in to your unreasonable demands, if you'll concede to my unacceptable offer.

Unionists are not afraid of work, look how they fight it.

I support the strike for shorter hours, sixty minutes is too long for an hour.

A faster assembly line is one thing, but why do we have to be sick before we take sick leave?

Of course time is money, but how much?

Striking school teachers have no class.

If the boss calls, be sure and get his name.

You need workers, I own workers. What am I bid?

If life was a bowl of cherries, the pickers would go on strike.

Save time, do it my way now instead of later.

Here they come, at a snail's pace.

Once upon a time and a half.

The strike is the weapon of the industrial jungle.

The results of next year's ballot have been stolen.

Union members drive to the picket line and then walk around in circles.

Unionists are steady workers. If they get any steadier, check for a pulse.

They cut our wages by five percent, but I managed to get it backdated to the beginning of the year.

If the servant grows rich and the master grows poor, they are both fit for nothing.

A wise unionist keeps those that hate him away from those that are undecided.

The union doesn't use its power to improve the quality of bad work, but to safeguard bad workers.

Strike, because all other means of communication will certainly fail.

You can only voice your opposition by rattling your chains.

Every boss needs adversity to keep him on his toes, that's why the union thoughtfully provides shop stewards.

He who divides, ultimately gets the worst share.

Do it by job, and you are under pressure to finish. Do it by the hour, and you have all the time in the world.

Their employer keeps asking for birth certificates, he wants to be sure they're still alive.

Agree with me now, it will save so much time later.

Don't fight a battle if you don't stand to gain anything by winning.

The less they have to do, the more time they need to do it in.

I'd like to compliment you on your work. When do you intend to start?

Debate is division in a union.

When they're not on strike or on holidays, teachers work during periods falling between pupil-free days.

Hang together, or hang separately.

You can tell a unionist by his hands, they're always in his pockets.

The strength of the union lies in its ability to bind its workers together.

The most effective labour saving device is a strike.

Unions have opened up new fields of unemployment.

Character

Character

There is good in the worst of us and bad in the best of us.

To reach greater heights, you need greater depth.

What is within is more important than what is without.

Character is worrying about your motives even when no-one is criticising you.

A stone thrown in the air is irresistibly drawn back to the ground where it belongs.

Character is destiny.

It's not how heavy the burden is, it's how strong your back is.

Snails and bulls both have horns, but different characters.

A crow goes abroad, and comes home just as black.

Better to make someone unhappy by doing right, than to make yourself unhappy by doing wrong.

The bamboo that bends is stronger than the oak that resists.

If you're interested in people, you meet exceptional people everywhere.

If it wasn't for caffeine, I'd have no personality whatsoever.

I try to go the extra mile, but someone always brings me back.

Character is the ability to stay on the level as you rise to the heights or plummet to the depths.

A well rounded character always gives others a square deal.

Character is the ability to decide for yourself.

You can't smell character unless it stinks.

Character is the ability to admire the qualities of those who achieve more than you do.

A change of scenery doesn't change your character.

What you don't run from, you learn from.

Character has a dual control system, operated by the head and the heart.

You are what you stand for, fall for, and believe in.

As he is in his heart, so he is.

Your character is defined by what amuses you and by what comforts you.

He's never failed to seek a peaceful solution after every other possibility has failed.

Nature breaks what it cannot bend.

You cannot rise above the reach of your character.

If you want to test a man's character, give him power.

Watch your habits, they become character.

Where a man is going is much more important than where he's been.

Character is much easier to keep than to recover.

The harder you fall, the higher you bounce.

Character begins when you start to wonder about your own motives.

A weak character is susceptible to influence.

Character is play their games, but biding by your own rules.

If you haven't got character, you need method and enthusiasm.

You're not a freak, you're a prototype.

Don't become the type of person your mother warned you against.

Some people are so conservative that they wear a seat belt in a drive-in movie.

Compromise erodes character.

Conformity

If you only sing in the chorus, your voice gets lost in the crowd.

The least cultivated taste has the largest appetite.

Conformity is the collective wisdom of individual ignorance.

The turtle makes no progress until he sticks his neck out.

People who stay in the middle of the road get run over.

Accepting what we are inhibits what we could become.

I can't keep pace, it's hard enough just staying in line.

Find out which way the crowd is going, and follow.

The toll is highest on the road least travelled.

You can't discover new oceans without losing sight of the shore.

Perhaps you're in the right cabin, but you're on the wrong ship.

In heaven, an angel is just another citizen.

Everyone saw the apple fall, but only Newton asked why.

Dead fish don't swim against the current.

If you must make trouble, try to make the sort that's socially acceptable.

If you can't keep pace, perhaps it's because you march to a different drummer.

Conformity allows the limited perception of others to define who we are.

The trouble with the rat race is that even when you win, you're still a rat.

When everybody thinks alike, propaganda is at it's most effective.

Obedience makes slaves of men.

A dead troublemaker is a live conformist.

If you're careful enough, nothing good or bad will ever happen to you.

You can draw on ruled paper if you want to.

The least intelligent obey the best.

A consistent thinker is an idiot who only knows how to repeat what he's heard before.

Everyone loves a neat category to slot others into.

Consistency isn't worth anything if you're consistently wrong.

Some people walk in the rain, and others just get wet.

Silence is consent in other words.

The man with the weird idea is a crank only until his idea succeeds.

Conformity means you have no faith in your ability to reason.

Watch your step. Everyone else is.

A rolling stone gathers no moss, but it does acquire a certain polish.

If you don't conform, you're abnormal, and if you're abnormal, you're despised.

Conformity is the ape of harmony.

Those who obey orders are not unhappy unless the orders go against the grain.

Stay in the rut and you won't run off the rails.

Conformity is the price of acceptance.

Arguments are always vulgar, and often convincing.

Trumpet with elephants, and bleat with goats.

Conformity is the sophistication of the modern ape in the concrete jungle.

Always take plenty of time to make a snap decision.

I'm cautious, he's a coward.

Mediocrity rises to the crest in a system that won't allow wave making.

It's easier to conform than it is to form your own judgement.

I used to get lost in the crowd, but now I crowd in with the lost.

Hypocrisy

Nice save, but you should beep when you back up like that.

If there's one thing a vulture can't stand, it's a glass eye.

Man is the only animal that stays on good terms with his prey until he intends to eat it.

I prefer those who render vice lovable, to those who degrade virtue.

Water takes the shape of the container it's in.

A hypocrite writes a book on atheism and asks his friends to pray it's a bestseller.

Deep down, he's shallow.

I can frame my face to all occasions.

Hypocrisy is prejudice with a halo.

Hypocrisy bites the hand that feeds it and licks the boot that kicks it.

When he takes off his face, you can see his mask.

For me? You shouldn't have. No really, you shouldn't have.

All great reformers of social injustice own several mansions themselves.

If you can't be good, imitate a good man.

A sanctimonious old iceberg who is waiting for a vacancy in the Holy Trinity.

Hypocrisy is sugar coated, but has a lemon filling.

The more someone has to be ashamed of, the more respectable he appears to be.

A hypocrite sells his soul and lives on the proceeds.

A hypocrite reads the bible to see if he can find a loophole.

The one who always agrees with you, always agrees with everyone else too.

A saint is a dead sinner who has been revised and edited.

A sickly saint is a healthy hypocrite.

When the fox preaches, look out for the geese.

There is no rogue like a religious rogue.

Actors are the only honest hypocrites.

Give a hypocrite enough time, and he will live up to his hypocrisy.

A hypocrite appreciates goodness enough to imitate it.

A humanitarian's family is always sadly neglected.

Better a friendly denial than an unwilling compliance.

No-one really likes a poor loser or a rich winner.

What shocks in public is practised in private.

Hypocrisy is the difference between promise and performance.

A hypocrite wipes tears off a mask.

He who serves two masters, serves one badly.

Join in the plan, but pity the man.

If you lead a double life, you will die more than one death.

Hypocrites are always willing to lend to those above them.

White gloves conceal dirty hands.

In a world where everything is ridiculous, nothing can be ridiculed.

Hypocrisy is the respect paid by vice to virtue.

Don't worry about being a hypocrite if you go to church, they always have room for one more.

Sometimes I'm the toilet, sometimes I'm the turd.

I am a deeply superficial person.

He doesn't kiss the boss's feet every day. Sometimes the boss is away.

Hypocrisy is a chameleon that turns whatever colour might be useful.

Reputation

If you lie down with dogs, you will get up with fleas.

I'm so ashamed, I'd kill myself, but what would people say?

Play with pigs, and people will suspect you of being one.

Nothing improves a reputation more than an obituary.

Reputation is what people say about you behind your back.

Confession may be good for the soul, but it plays havoc with the reputation.

Reputation is your good name, with whatever you've been caught doing, subtracted from it.

You can never retrieve a good name once you've lost it.

As his name is, so is he.

Slander murders a reputation.

Reputation is the high price of self-ownership.

A good reputation is when they don't find you out what you did until after you die.

We value ourselves above others, and yet we consider their opinion more important than our own.

If only I could be respected, without having to be respectable too.

With such a bad name, how can anyone insult you?

You can call it a shovel, but a spade is a spade.

Every cask smells of the wine it once contained.

Some people wouldn't recognise their own reputations if they met.

Secretive men have good reputations.

A bad reputation is when your wicked past catches up with you.

When we find out what someone really thinks of us, it only confirms what we've always thought of them.

The reputation of a lifetime can be determined by the conduct of a single hour.

Reputation is the praise you received from honest men, and the abuse of rogues.

A good reputation means others aren't thinking about you.

Those whose reputations the gods wish to destroy, they first call promising.

All dead people are good.

You need a good reputation to get the job, but you need ability to keep it.

As reputation increases, ability declines.

A reputation is like a shadow, it follows you wherever you go.

If you live with a cripple, you learn to limp.

A good name keeps shining even in the dark.

I am better than my reputation would lead you to believe.

Reputation is often obtained without merit and lost without fault.

A bad reputation gets there before you do.

If you have a reputation as an early riser, you can stay in bed till noon.

I'm not as bad as they say I am.

The reputations of big men make big targets.

Never do anything you wouldn't be caught dead doing.

There is no reputation so secure that gossip can't taint it.

You can't get rid of the old pages by turning over a new leaf.

A good reputation is proof that your neighbours mind their own business.

If only I'd had the time and energy to do all the things they say I've done.

Danger

Accidents

Don't drive faster than your guardian angel can fly.

I had been driving for nearly thirty years before I fell asleep at the wheel.

The lighter the head, the heavier the foot.

I wasn't driving too fast, I was flying too low.

So many pedestrians, so little time.

A careful driver always slows down before going through a red light.

Go on green, stop on red, and slow down when I turn white.

Don't learn the road rules by accident.

Here lies Les, who watched the ads. No Les, no more.

You can tell how much faith a man has in God by the way he drives.

Being too cautious is the greatest risk of all.

I intend to break the speed record, or die trying.

If your wife wants to drive, don't stand in her way.

Most great discoveries were made by accident.

He who groans loudest is least hurt.

Horse power has replaced horse sense.

Some people seem to have accidents just waiting in ambush for them.

Dozens of bolts hold a car together, but a lone nut can scatter it all over the place.

To get to the nearest hospital, drive the wrong way down a one way.

A truck backed through my windshield into my face.

He was all over the road and I had to swerve a number of times before I hit him.

Cars eliminated the need for horses and now they're working on people.

The worst part of any accident is when someone says, *I told you so.*

If your bumper sticker wasn't so small, I wouldn't have to drive so close to read it.

It's not speed that kills, it's the sudden stop.

The overtaker's side is on the right, the undertaker's side is on the left.

Two wrongs won't make a right, but three rights make a left.

Loose nuts hit and run, and then they bolt.

Proceed by plan, be hit by accident.

Maybe you'll like the ambulance's safety belts better.

Accident is the greatest of all inventors.

I'm faster than a speeding ticket.

Be an angel and let me drive. And he did, and he is.

Drive like lightning and you'll crash like thunder.

Drive carefully, the life you save could be that of someone you love.

The bag with the eggs in it is the one that will drop.

Fortunately for us, the greatest traffic hazard is becoming easier to eliminate, the pedestrian.

If you're not a haemorrhoid, get off my backside.

If that wasn't a large black cat with a white collar, we've just run over the vicar.

When you've mastered the use of your indicators, you can go back to saving the whale..

You never learn to swear until you learn to drive.

Speeding can change your naughty brats into sweet little angels permanently.

Courage

Courage extends to those parts that alcohol can't reach.

It doesn't take a brave dog to bark at a lion's bones.

You can't act courageously unless you're scared to death.

Courage is the difference between keeping your chin up and sticking your neck out.

Courage is merely a theory until it's tested.

If you're brave too often, people will come to expect it of you.

It's a brave mouse that breeds in a cat's ear.

It takes courage to say what you think, and it's lonely.

Courage is being careless about your life in order to keep it.

It's easy to be brave from a safe distance.

Sometimes there's no difference between courage and the thrill of excitement.

The guts carry the feet, and the feet carry the guts.

If you alone have kept your head, it's because you have no comprehension of the trouble you're in.

I haven't even begun to fight yet.

Everyone dies, but not everyone lives.

Few are courageous without witnesses.

Courage is the knowledge that the enemy is a coward.

Courage is three parts whiskey, one part water.

If it's worth having, it's worth fighting for.

Courage doesn't always march to a bugle.

A man is a lion for his own cause.

A brave man will always respond to a high reward.

Courage is the ability to keep your fear locked within.

Courage is a test of virtue.

Courage is the ability to suspend imagination.

Bravery is being the only one who knows how frightened you are.

You always have courage, at least until you find you actually need it.

Courage is fear that hasn't surrendered yet.

A timid person is frightened before, a coward during, and a hero, after.

Courage stems from character under pressure.

Courage rises to the occasion.

Courage is a strong desire to live, disguised as a willingness to die.

Nerve succeeds.

Courage is not the absence of fear, but the ability to overcome that fear.

It is more courageous to say no, than to go ahead with something stupid just to impress others.

Courage is the willingness to endure fear.

A hero is a fool who thinks he's invincible.

Courage is forethought.

I'm not going to let them scare me.

Keep your fears to yourself, but share your courage.

Courage atrophies from lack of use.

Courage demands a temporary surrender of security.

There's no such thing as courage, there are only degrees of fear.

It takes courage to be gentle when there is violence all around you.

Courage is fear that has said its prayers.

Crime

Organised crime is the only business the government doesn't meddle in.

Crime is a shady business that enables you to buy a fabulous place in the sun.

A drug runner has no respect for other countries' customs.

Every criminal finds God in the shadow of the gallows.

Prison reform will never work until they start stocking our prisons with a better class of criminal.

Of course crime pays, it's the biggest business in the world.

Spare me a few dollars, all I have in the world is this knife I'm holding at your throat.

A forger produces money you can't bank on.

The fish that opens its mouth is the one that gets caught.

The police do not exist to create disorder, they are there to preserve disorder.

Crime doesn't always pay, but the hours are good.

A bribe is when the giver says *Thanks*, and the receiver says *Don't mention it.*

Trust in the Lord, but get a good lawyer.

I started out as an unwanted child, but now I'm wanted all over Australia.

Crime breeds on diluted punishment.

Bad cop. No donut.

It's not that thieves don't respect other people's property, it's just that they want to respect it on their own premises.

Some are born good, some make good, and some are caught with the goods.

I've earned everything I've got through my job as a thief.

No-one steals a big screen television set so that his family can enjoy better viewing.

The culprit makes the first accusation.

It is better not to accuse than to acquit the guilty.

He who excuses himself, accuses himself.

Follow in your family's fingerprints.

You cannot wash blood off your hands.

Old burglars never die, they just steal away into the night.

Crime is the logical extension of legitimate business.

I'm not against the police, I'm just scared to death of them.

Prevention of crime depends on the certainty of punishment.

Today's rogue is tomorrow's hero.

The crab teaches its young to walk straight, like itself.

Whoever profits from the crime is guilty of it.

Criminals are go-getters in the process of solving the crime of poverty.

Little thieves hang while great ones escape.

Legalise crime and tax it out of existence.

Am I my brother's copper?

The cops couldn't track an elephant in the snow, even if it had a nosebleed.

The Mafia has turned crime into a spectator sport.

In the old days, the punishment used to fit the crime.

All theft relies on a receiver.

To eradicate crime, it should be nationalised so it will start running at a loss.

He's so crooked that if he swallowed a nail, he would shit a corkscrew.

The world is neither flat nor round, it's crooked.

Stolen fruit is always sweeter.

Danger

Those who live on the edge are just begging to be pushed off.

When you're in deep water, keep your mouth shut.

Never squat while wearing spurs.

There's nothing more exhilarating than a lucky escape.

There is safety in insignificance.

There is always free cheese in the mouse trap.

No guts, no glory.

Never draw fire, it irritates those around you.

In skating over thin ice, there is safety in speed.

Always pack your own parachute.

To conquer without danger is to triumph without glory.

Never call a crocodile a big mouth before you're safely passed him.

Danger breeds best on overconfidence.

You have to overcome the boar's sharp tusks to obtain the meat.

Look for trouble and you will find it.

A life of danger diminishes the dread of death.

Anticipation is worse that the act.

Everyone loves the excitement of a burning house when it isn't theirs.

AIDS has made sex more dangerous than the cigarette afterwards.

No-one pities the snake charmer when the cobra strikes him.

We thrive on the danger we see others in.

Never stand between the dog and the fire hydrant.

In the greatest danger, the most outrageous plan is most likely to succeed.

Women do not like timid men, as cats do not like prudent mice.

There is nobody for whom somebody is not dangerous.

Stick your neck out far enough, and someone will lop it off.

Life without danger is a waste of oxygen.

It isn't as dangerous to treat a man badly as it is to treat him well.

It's not danger we fear, but the fear of danger.

If you pause to worry about danger, fear grows.

It's a small step from anticipation to terror.

Without danger, the game grows cold.

Self-preservation is the first law of nature.

A good scare is worth more than any advice.

We are all dangerous until our thoughts make us fearful.

In danger, courage endangers life.

We are as brave as we need to be when the occasion arises.

They sicken of the calm who know the storm.

Danger is sweetened by risk.

However stable the foundation is, life is always risky.

I think, therefore I'm dangerous.

Sometimes it's better to dive out of a window than to wait for the fire to reach you.

We don't want safety from danger as much as we want immunity from fear.

Danger past, God is packed away until next time.

The storm of thought stimulates more than the calm of ignorance.

Bravery is not necessarily an act of courage.

Fear

Better a coward briefly than a dead hero forever.

Longevity is the ultimate manifestation of fear.

Fear is a roller coaster that speeds up in the dark.

If you are afraid of nothing, you instil fear in others.

When you're afraid, everything rustles in the dark.

There is nothing in the dark that wasn't there when the light was on.

A person trying to hide never thinks he is sufficiently concealed.

The weight of the burden varies according to the bearer.

A coward is a family man with a mortgage.

Cowards threaten only when they feel safe.

If you're in danger, assess the situation carefully and act only if bravery is beneficial.

Fear has the biggest eyes and ears of all.

He who rides a tiger is afraid to dismount.

Bullies are cowards who have the temporary courage to make others afraid too.

Amongst every ten men, nine are likely to be women.

I could be a coward, if only I had the courage of my convictions.

A coward is someone with a normally developed instinct for self preservation.

Never fear shadows, it means there is light nearby.

Heroes are people who ignore their personal responsibilities.

Suffering has limits, fear has none.

As cowardly as a coward is, it isn't wise to call him a coward.

Cowards are only willing to fight those who will not reciprocate.

You are not brave because you are too afraid to run away.

I am cautious, but you are a coward.

A coward is a summer soldier and a sunshine patriot.

A coward thinks with his legs.

The love of power overcomes cowardice.

Most anticipation instils some degree of cowardice.

Cowardice is caused by an overactive imagination.

Make others live in fear and sooner or later, they will retaliate.

Cold feet rarely accompany a cool head.

No-one is brave without witnesses.

Fear is pain arising from the anticipation of evil.

Oh, for the wings of a bird that could fly away.

Fear slows down thinking and speeds up running.

A runaway monk never speaks well of his monastery.

A coward dies a thousand times before his death.

A man can be killed by his own courage.

He'd commit suicide if he wasn't afraid of killing himself.

I have no physical defects, but I have no guts.

As spineless as spaghetti.

There is no such thing as bravery, only degrees of fear.

If God wanted us to be brave, why did he give us legs?

If you suffer from a complete lack of imagination, you're afraid of nothing.

A coward prefers to describe himself as a cautious man.

You don't have to conquer the mountain, just your fear of it.

Violence

We need more guns like we need a hole in the head.

Survivors will be prosecuted.

It's not the bullet with my name on it that worries me, it's the one that says *to whom it may concern.*

Keep honking, I'm just busy reloading.

Violence is the need of the mentally weak to prove they are physically strong.

It isn't the size of the dog in the fight, it's the size of the fight in the dog.

Whosoever shall smite thee on thy right cheek, flatten him.

Would you like to step outside and say that? Good, now I can talk in peace.

I will defend myself, because I would rather be judged by twelve than carried by six.

Guns don't kill people, people with guns kill people.

If you love something, set it free. If it doesn't come back, hunt it down and kill it.

Have gun, will massacre.

I use my fists because I'm too stupid to use my brain.

Violence never solves the problem permanently.

The bigger they are, the harder they hit.

A black eye is a stamp of disapproval.

Guns are not safe even when you're safely behind the barrel.

A meaningless collective guilt has replaced a meaningful individual responsibility.

A lion never lies down with the lamb, unless the lamb is inside the lion.

Violence is the manifestation of impotence.

When barricades close the streets, detours become the way to go.

Man is far worse than any animal when he acts like an animal.

Violence is essentially wordless.

Violence is the force used when persuasion fails.

Never mind the dog, beware of the owner.

You can attack if you like, I'm insured by Smith & Wesson.

You cannot peacefully maintain what you have acquired through force.

The law prohibits the use of force by anyone, except the law.

A little violence can get you lots of stuff.

Keep violence in the mind, where it belongs.

An articulate voice is no competition for fists.

I am more afraid of a stray bullet than I am of a random knife attack.

Any excuse serves a violent man.

Disembowelling takes guts.

The violent fall to violence.

The best form of defence is offence.

Violence is the clothing covering the nakedness of impotence.

If an armed man wants to hurt you but his gun won't fire, he'll hit you with it.

When one man hits another, it means a fool has lost his argument.

Violence is the last refuge of the incompetent.

The one who strikes first has run out of words.

Guns don't kill people, irate husbands who come home unexpectedly do.

Even when you've overcome an enemy by force, his mind is still free.

Do not expect justice where might is right.

Man eats the big fish, and the big fish eats the little fish.

Eloquence

Advice

Advice is free, and it's worth every cent.

Always heed a friend's advice, it makes them feel so much better.

An Eskimo can easily advise an Arab on how to cope with a heat wave.

We should swap problems, since you obviously know how to solve mine.

We give advice by the bucket and take it by the grain.

Sometimes even a fool can make a good suggestion.

Never walk when you can ride.

Advice is ninety nine percent sound, and one percent counsel.

Those who are wise enough to give good advice, are sensible enough not to.

When someone asks you for advice, they usually let you know how they want you to decide.

The worst men give the best advice.

No matter how bad advice is, it never harms before it is implemented.

The best advice is found on the pillow in the morning.

The best cure for insomnia is plenty of sleep.

Advice generally pleases more than it helps.

He who takes advice is superior to him that gives it.

Advice is a laxative, easy to take, but with dire consequences.

The only time to be positive is when you're certain you're wrong.

Advice is the elderly's compensation for their inability to set a bad example.

A good example beats any advice.

No matter how thin you slice it, it's still baloney.

Any fool can offer advice, and most fools do.

A word to the wise usually causes resentment.

Advice after the event is as useful as medicine administered after death.

Second thoughts are always wiser.

If you're not rich, pretend you're wise.

When we are well, we are full of advice for the ill.

Whatever your advice, keep it brief.

Listen to advice, but act according to your own judgement.

We can give advice but we cannot inspire conduct.

He who has no children, brings them up well.

When all is said and done, more is said.

You cheat yourself when you take advice that was given free.

Build according to advice, and you will have a very crooked house.

Advice is offered for much less than it was paid for.

A drop of example is worth an ocean of advice.

When in doubt, give advice.

Bought advice is worth twice as much as free advice.

Never trust the judgement of a man in difficulty himself.

Advice is what we ask for when we already know the answer, but wish we didn't.

When you ask someone for advice, you really just want an accomplice.

The trouble with giving advice is that people want to repay you.

Don't hesitate to give advice. It helps to pass the time, and no-one listens anyway.

Conversation

How am I supposed to have a decent conversation when you keep talking?

The opposite of talking is waiting for your turn.

Drawing on my fine command of language, I said nothing.

If we interrupt others to display our own knowledge, we parade our ignorance.

Don't express yourself more clearly than you can think.

The voice is a second face.

God gave us two ears and one mouth, the idea being that we should listen more than we speak.

We never really listen, because we are too eager to speak.

The shorter the gospel, the longer the sermon.

Let's get to know each other better before we complicate our relationship by trying to communicate in depth.

Of all the things I've lost, I miss my memory the most.

The thoughtless are never wordless.

Some people get unlimited mileage out of a limited vocabulary.

The mouth is faster than the mind.

The thought got run over as it was crossing my mind.

I've just spent two hours talking to her for a few minutes.

Don't talk to me while I'm interrupting.

If you listened properly the first time, you might have heard what I meant to say.

Even with so many subjects to choose from, some of us still can't meet a paraplegic without talking about cripples.

What the heart is full of, escapes through the mouth.

There is nothing worse than the sharp image of a fuzzy concept.

Your ignorance cramps my conversation.

We try our thoughts on others to assess their value.

The art of conversation is about hearing, as well as being heard.

I'm a good listener. God knows, I've had enough practice.

Your words don't decide what you're going to say, you do.

I know she can be outspoken, but I've never met anyone who could do it.

Talk is cheap because supply exceeds demand.

Think twice before you speak, and everybody is already talking about something else.

Silence isolates, speech consolidates.

It's great to hold a conversation, but it should be set free now and again.

Thought corrupts language, and language corrupts thought.

Silence is the ultimate expression of contempt.

The agony in an animal's eyes conveys more than words.

Conversation is the art of being obscure clearly.

A tongue is soft and yet it can cut like a knife.

Don't talk unless you can improve the silence.

Profanity is the trade mark of the conversational cripple.

Think twice before you speak, so that you can say something really nasty.

In conversation, discretion is more important than eloquence.

Talking isn't about communication, everyone's too busy to pay much attention.

Youth is silent, the old repeat themselves, and the boredom is mutual.

A good ear can stand bad words.

Flattery

Chew it over, enjoy the taste, but never swallow it.

Man does not live by bread alone, he needs buttering up.

Flattery is the art of stroking someone's mind with your tongue.

I can live for two months on a good compliment.

A word of encouragement during failure is worth a dictionary of praise after success.

Flattery is like perfume, it should be smelled but never swallowed.

The thicker the fog, the louder the horn.

Praise loudly, blame softly.

If we did not flatter ourselves, we would be immune to the flattery of others.

Tell me if you notice me doing everything right.

Flattery makes good men better and bad men worse.

Compliments are embarrassing because they never go far enough.

It makes you feel good because everyone knows how much you deserve it.

Flattery is the applause that refreshes.

Flattery is allowed to stay long after plain talking has been kicked out.

Flattery publicly embarrasses me, but I secretly love it.

Some people have to die to be praised.

If you want to lick the bowl, flatter the cook.

I would have flattered you more had you flattered me less.

Modesty is the triumph of mind over flatter.

Flattery corrupts the giver and the receiver.

Flattery is like having Dracula admire your neck.

The deafest man can still hear praise.

Say it now, because a dead man can't read his own tombstone.

The advantage of flattering yourself is that you can lay it on thick in exactly the right places.

I would rather be hurt by flattery than helped by criticism.

We only despise flattery when it's directed at others.

Whenever the occasion rose, he rose to the occasion.

He who refutes praise is actually asking for more.

A love of flattery stems from a high opinion of yourself.

Anybody can be flattered, simply by telling them they're not the type who can be flattered.

It's flattering even when we're not deceived by it.

Compliments cost nothing, yet we sometimes pay dearly for them.

Flattery is praise that you didn't earn.

Most people can't tell the difference between sugar and artificial sweeteners.

Of course flattery is poison, but it intoxicates.

Flattery is what makes a husband out of a bachelor.

You catch more flies with honey than you do with vinegar.

Everybody believes a liar when he says sweet things.

Flattery will get you everywhere.

It's easier to flatter someone into something than it is to bully them out of it.

Some people pay compliments as though they expect a receipt.

Blarney is flattery laid on so thin that you can't help but love it.

Flattery is fine as long as you don't inhale.

Gossip

He who throws mud loses ground.

A monologue is one woman talking, a 'catologue' is two women talking.

The hearing ear is usually found near the wagging tongue.

Great minds discuss ideas, small minds discuss people.

To make a mountain out of a molehill, just add dirt.

Sticks and stones are nothing compared to the hurt words can cause.

A gossip always has enough spare time to attend to other people's business.

If you can't say anything good about anyone, come sit here by me.

A secret is something some people just can't wait to tell.

Always start the rumours yourself, otherwise you have no way of knowing whether they're true or not.

Nothing carries gossip faster than a sour grapevine.

I've already told you more than I know myself.

The narrowest minds have the widest mouths.

It's easier to tell secrets in the dark.

Gossips should be seen but not heard.

Have a friend and keep her such, but never let her know too much.

Women gossip, but men trade secrets for benefits.

An abundance of words usually accompanies poverty of thought.

That little birdie that told you is a stool pigeon.

Of course three people can keep a secret, but only if two are already dead.

Only a parrot repeats what it hears without trying to make it seem better.

The eyes and ears represent four information inlets, the mouth the only information exit. Just another crazy coincidence?

If you're breaking glass, don't walk barefoot.

I heard it out of the corner of her mouth.

Twenty percent fact, eighty percent fiction.

As plain as the tip of your tongue.

Those who repeat secrets separate friends.

There's nothing worse than being talked about, except being ignored.

Scandal is gossip made tedious by morality.

Don't burn your mouth tasting other people's soup.

The person who knows nothing soon repeats it in vindictive whispers.

A closed mouth catches no feet.

Gossip gallops while discretion dithers along.

Reality has a nasty habit of squashing really good rumours.

The worse it is, the better it is.

Hearsay, smearsay.

Your business is my business, is his business, is her business.

An idle person's tongue is never idle.

Walk on water, and people will say it's because you don't know how to swim.

Secrets are a burden, which is why most people want help to carry them.

Never tell a lie if the truth will do more damage.

Those who gossip to you soon gossip about you.

When mud is thrown it doesn't always stick, but it leaves a dirty mark.

Language

The dictionary has a fine vocabulary, but not much of a plot.

Always proof read your work to see whether you might have any words out.

Is there a word that contains all the vowels? Unquestionably.

Speak, so that I can see you.

Language experts believe the exclamation mark should be deleted from punctuation, because no-one's surprised at anything anymore.

In the beginning, and the word was *aardvark.*

Words are versatile instruments which can be as soothing as music or as inflaming as an inferno.

Words can never express what they cannot express.

A poor listener never hears a worthwhile conversation.

The shortest distance between two puns is the straight line.

There are people who talk at you, and not to you.

Every country has its own laugh.

Language is the pedigree of the nation.

England and America are separated by the same language.

Even if you're not a good conversationalist, you can still be a great listener.

If you can't communicate, at least shut up about it.

The philosophy of our ancestors is still audible in our everyday modern language.

Slang is the language that rolls up its sleeves, spits on its hands, and goes to work.

Nothing emphasises a lack of vocabulary more than swear words.

Words are an assault of thought by the unthinking.

I am a bear of very little brain, and long words bother me.

They also serve who only punctuate.

The two most beautiful words in any language are *cheque enclosed.*

A synonym is the word you use when you can't spell the word you originally wanted to use.

Fact is richer than diction.

French is for diplomats, Spanish is for lovers, and Italian is for singers.

Never use a big word when a diminutive one will suffice.

An adjective is the banana peel of parts of speech.

And whose cruel idea was it to put the 'S' into lisp?

Man does not live by words alone, although he sometimes has to eat them.

If is the biggest word in the English language.

When in doubt, delete the adjective.

Yesterday I couldn't spell educated, now I are it.

Who makes a pun, picks a pocket.

Whenever you speak, your mind is on display.

Dyslexics of the world untie.

Why does monosyllable have so many syllables?

Lies

I've asked you a thousand times, don't exaggerate.

There is nothing so insignificant that it cannot be blown out of all proportion.

An excuse is a thin layer of maybe covering a blatant lie.

One small lie can destroy a whole reputation for integrity.

A person who never lies has no consideration for other's feelings.

The truth is merely the lie that is the easiest to believe.

It's not so much that he exaggerates, it's just that he remembers big.

There are no lies so reckless that they lack all support.

Half the lies they tell about me aren't true.

An excuse is a problem that has grown into a lie.

A drop of inaccuracy saves a bucket of explanation.

A lie is an abomination to the Lord, and a great help in times of trouble.

A lie by some other name is what makes mushrooms grow.

A lie makes sense when the truth endangers.

For every credibility gap there is a credibility fill.

He occasionally stumbled over the truth, but picked himself up and hurried on as though nothing had happened.

The liar's punishment is that he always suspects everyone else of lying too.

I reserve the right to contradict everything I say today, tomorrow.

Lie for me, and I'll lie for you.

A bad excuse diminishes the value of all the good excuses you offered before.

Start with a white lie and pretty soon you're colour blind.

While our lips can still move, we will continue to lie.

A multitude of words cloaks a single lie.

The best lie is a little one that goes a long way.

That little white lie soon grows into a tanned adult.

Good morning, he lied.

Never offer an excuse you wouldn't be willing to accept yourself.

No liar has a good enough memory.

A conviction is a far more dangerous enemy of the truth than a lie.

If he's willing to lie for you, he's willing to lie against you.

A lie cannot support itself, it needs other lies to prop it up.

A clever liar gives no details.

Ask no questions and you'll be told no lies.

The handwriting on the wall is a forgery.

Without lies, we would die of boredom.

Truth that's told with a bad intention is more evil than any lie you can invent.

I wouldn't believe him if he said he was lying.

You can get away with ninety-nine lies, but the hundredth will betray you.

There aren't enough crutches for the world's lame excuses.

A lie looks better if it has a witness.

A lie can travel around the world while the truth is still putting on its shoes.

A legend is a lie that has attained the dignity of age.

One lie will give birth to ten others.

There is nothing more pathetic than a forgetful liar.

Quotations

Avoid clichés like the plague.

A proverb is a short sentence based on long experience.

Proverbs are invaluable treasures to dunces with good memories.

A quote is a profound thought imprisoned until an equal mind sets it free.

A good quote is its own reword.

You can be witty with someone else's wit, but you cannot be wise with their wisdom.

One man's wit is another man's quotation.

I wish I'd said that. Ah, you will, you will.

Famous remarks are seldom quoted correctly.

Quotations enable us to be smart with someone else's mind.

It's all been said before, but nobody ever listens.

Proverbs are the currency of human experience.

The surest way to make a monkey out of a man is to quote him.

A quotation whose time has come is stronger than an army.

What I say today, the world will say tomorrow.

The proverb is to speech what spice is to life.

A witty person merely says what you would say if you had thought of it first.

I shall never be ashamed of citing a bad author if the line is good.

I'd rather be quotable than boring.

Someone who makes puns should be drawn and quoted.

What the first philosopher taught, the last will repeat.

The malice of a good thing is the barb that makes it stick.

Little quotes have sharp edges.

Constant quotations will make you a byword yourself.

You can judge a man by his favourite quotations.

Hold fast to the words of your ancestors.

I hate quotations. Tell me what you know.

Hush little bright line don't you cry, you'll be a cliché by and by.

No proverb is a proverb to you until life has illustrated it.

I couldn't have said it better myself.

Maxims are the condensed common sense of nations.

Next to being witty yourself, the next best thing is being able to quote another's wit.

I often quote myself. It adds spice to my conversation.

One man's wit is another man's wisdom.

The profoundest thought is imprisoned until an equal mind sets it free.

A good quote never goes out of fashion.

The wisdom of the wise and the experience of the ages are perpetuated by quotations.

A gift for quotation is a serviceable substitute for wit.

What people quote reveals what they think.

Proverbs represent the philosophy of the common people.

Now we sit through Shakespeare in order to recognise the quotations.

Its body should be brevity, its soul wit.

Wise sayings fall on barren ground, but a kind word is never thrown away.

Let's have some new clichés.

Proverbs condense into a sentence what has taken years to learn.

Speeches

Be sincere, be brief, be seated.

Be sure your brain is engaged before putting your mouth in gear.

I know there's someone out there, I can hear them coughing.

Some speeches revolutionise the concept of eternity.

Accustomed as I am to public speaking, I know how bored you all must be.

The object of the speech is not truth, but persuasion.

Exhaust neither the subject nor the audience.

When his mouth opens, his head empties.

The problem with most speeches is that bad weather keeps the best people away.

He devoted the best years of his life to preparing his impromptu speeches.

It takes us years to learn to talk, and yet we lose the ability the instant we're asked to give a speech.

A good speech is like a pencil, it has to have a sharp point.

A speech should have a good beginning and a good ending, and the two should be close together.

If it goes without saying, let it.

When the listening begins to lessen, you've overdone it.

Some men are masters at saying nothing, very slowly.

Some people tell you they're no good at public speaking, then spend an hour convincing you they didn't exaggerate.

Public speaking requires audience participation.

Be sincere, whether you mean it or not.

Oratory is the art of making many empty words sound like deep thoughts.

No speech that's very short is altogether bad.

Occasional flashes of silence make his speech perfectly delightful.

Do not open your mouth before your brain is in gear.

If it weren't for Churchill's speeches, we would be speaking German today.

A good speech shouldn't come to a bad ending.

The object of my words is to conceal my thoughts.

To speak without thinking is like firing without aiming.

He missed an invaluable opportunity to sit down and shut up.

He is inebriated by the exuberance of his own verbosity.

Anyway, that's neither here nor funny.

Not only does he lack the ability to speak well, but he doesn't know when to shut up.

Making a speech is diluting a two minute idea with a thirty minute vocabulary.

Those who lack the power of speech have the gift of intelligence.

He shoots from the lip.

Make them laugh, and when their mouths open, you stuff something in quickly.

They generally give speeches after dinner, so that you can blame that pain on indigestion.

One dumb at one end, many numb at the other.

He makes you wish you were deaf.

Clothes disguise him, but words reveal him.

Some have eloquence and some have brains.

Speech is the art of talking humorously without saying anything.

And here's another one you're going to hate.

Truth

Of course the truth hurts, anything that has been stretched that much would hurt.

Truth is perception, and everyone's is different.

Always tell the truth, even if you have to lie a little to do it.

He can't tell the truth without lying.

One lie can distort a thousand truths.

Truth is violated by lies, and outraged by silence.

Honesty is almost always the best policy.

An incredible truth is rarely believed.

Nothing stops us from learning the truth as much as the belief that we already know it.

No-one wants to hear a truth that violates his convictions.

If you tell the truth, there's less to remember.

Never believe another liar even if you know he's telling the truth.

Truth is a tiny island surrounded by lies.

Better a lie that soothes than a truth that hurts.

If you want to convey misinformation, tell the truth.

If telling the truth is so good, how come no-one wants to hear it?

Truth needs no crutches. If it limps, it's a lie.

Whatever you believe to be true, becomes the truth.

The credit gained by the lie lasts only until the truth comes out.

Truth is stranger than fiction, to some people.

To believe with certainty, we must begin by doubting.

I have abandoned my search for the truth, and settled for a good fantasy.

Truth can be stretched but it cannot be broken.

Sometimes you have to betray someone else in order to be true to yourself.

The one who always agrees with you, always agrees with everyone else too.

If you want to tell the truth, leave elegance to the tailor.

The truth is more important than the facts.

The problem with a half-truth is that you can never be sure which half you possess.

A half-truth is a whole lie.

Truth is the most persuasive argument.

Give a man a mask, and he'll tell you the truth.

The worst people always think it's their duty to tell you the hurtful truth.

Truth is not hypothesis turned to fact.

He tells the truth as often as the weather bureau.

Doubt is an invitation to think about the truth.

If truth barks at the heels of error, it will get its head kicked in.

Honest answers increase anxiety.

Truth springs from arguments amongst friends.

I have seen the truth and it makes no sense.

Repetition can transform a lie into the truth.

Any fool can tell the truth, but it takes a clever man to lie well.

Speak the truth, but leave immediately after.

Some circumstantial evidence is convincing, like when you find a trout in the milk.

Tell the truth, but allow it to lean a little.

The greater the truth, the worse the libel.

Endurance

Adversity

Mosquitoes never sleep.

Every dog should have fleas, it keeps him from brooding about being a dog.

Don't exaggerate your problems, it's easier to climb a molehill than a mountain.

My downfall raises me to infinite heights.

The engine won't start and the payments won't stop.

When life gives you lemons, make lemonade.

Only the man swimming knows exactly how strong the current is.

I wept because I had no shoes, and then I met a man who had no feet.

You need to know what's bitten you before you can take the antidote.

Just when I was getting used to yesterday, along came today.

The greatest pleasure in life is doing what everyone said couldn't be done.

If you're pouring concrete, there will be a cloudburst.

The severity of the itch is proportionate to the inaccessibility of the spot.

I respect faith, but doubt is what gets you ahead.

A good solution can be applied to almost any problem.

A shoelace never breaks while it's being tied.

Great fleas have little fleas on their backs to bite them.

We never put our best foot forward until we've burnt the other one in hot water.

When an elephant is in trouble, even an ant will kick him.

We risk becoming the best informed society that ever died of ignorance.

It's not what they take away from you, it's what you do with what's left that counts.

The shortest route between two points is always under repair.

There is nothing the body suffers that the mind does not benefit by.

Unless you've suffered deprivation yourself, how can you know the extent of your own depravity?

If there were no winter, no-one would appreciate spring.

Tears are the heart's safety valves.

A drowning man doesn't worry about a little rain.

A man can only be demolished by himself.

If it doesn't kill you, it makes you stronger.

Financial adversity is what distinguishes man from other beasts.

The worse the voyage, the more welcome the port.

The mouse doesn't want the cheese any more, he just wants to get out of the trap.

Great crises produce great men.

If you want to jump high, you have to make a long run.

It's all over bar the shouting.

If you're not riding the wave of change, you're about to get dumped under it.

How can I have come so far, and yet still have so far to go?

Every path has a puddle.

If someone didn't upset the apple cart, the apples would rot.

If I seem to be running, perhaps it's because I'm being pursued.

When the going gets tough, the tough get going.

Adversity is something you rise above.

It's easy to bear another's adversity.

Affliction refines some and consumes others.

Experience

Experience is how we learn how stupid we've been.

The old horse knows the way.

There's no fool like an old fool, and that's why you can't beat experience.

It's so simple that a five year old, with twenty years' experience, could do it.

Experience is what happens after that fine print you didn't read.

Experience rises from the ruins of illusion.

If you can't get ahead on your own strengths, learn from the weaknesses of others.

The questions I ask myself arise as a result of someone else's experience.

Experience is a light that allows us to see where we have gone wrong.

It's disgraceful to stub your toe against the same stone twice.

Some speak from experience and others, from experience, are silent.

Experience is the many speed bumps on the road to perfection.

History is prophecy from behind.

We carry our experience through life like excess baggage.

Listen to others, because you already know what you're going to say.

A man who carries a cat by the tail learns something he can learn no other way.

Experience is what enables you to recognise a mistake when you make it again.

Experience only teaches the teachable.

It takes just a moment in childhood to cross the threshold in adulthood.

It's feeling the pain long after the injury.

No man's knowledge goes beyond his experience.

Experience is what makes you examine your idiocy, but only after you've been had.

Good judgement comes from experience, and experience comes from bad judgement.

Experience is what life hands you, growth is optional.

Experience asks questions first, and when the test is over, tells you the answers.

One thorn of experience is worth a wilderness of warning.

If you don't learn from hard knocks, you become a soft touch.

Experience either makes you bitter or better.

If we shake hands with icy fingers, it's because we've been burnt before.

Experience is the name we give our mistakes.

Only the wearer knows where the shoe pinches.

Experience lets us admit our mistakes before others exaggerate them.

Experience is no substitute for intelligence.

Scalded cats fear even cold water.

Experience is how you use what happens to you.

Experience is when you remember the destination, but forget the route.

An old poacher makes the best gamekeeper.

Experience teaches us that truth is ever changing.

If you don't drink from the spring of experience, you'll die of thirst in the desert of ignorance.

Experience shows us the path we should have taken.

Good judgement comes from bad experience.

A drunk doesn't necessarily make a good bartender.

Our feet are guided by the path of experience.

Experience is the awful thing you get when you were expecting something wonderful.

Stress

Stress occurs because some people don't know how to worry without getting upset.

I'm not stressed out. I sleep like a baby, every two hours I wake up and cry.

I can't relax, tension is all that holds me together.

A diamond is a chunk of coal that made good under pressure.

Patience my arse, I'm going to kill something.

I've had just about all I can stand of myself.

Don't let stress kill you, let God help.

Stress is the art of constantly replacing one worry with another.

Since corporate stress seminars began, production is down and nobody cares.

What weighs on my mind grates on my nerves.

Do not disturb? I'm already disturbed.

Stress is when you climb Mount Everest without even being there.

There can't be another crisis, my schedule is full.

Stress is the interval between now and then.

Stress is the inability to dread one day at a time.

Sometimes I get an almost overwhelming desire to go on living.

Stress leave has brought nervous breakdowns within the reach of public servants.

Stress is man's unspoken criticism of nature's uncertainty.

Solitude is the mother of anxiety.

Stress is when the trivial matters acquire a peculiar importance of their own.

I have no mouth and I need to scream.

Stress is when an adult feels as frustrated and confused as a baby in a topless bar.

Stress is the inability to enjoy a crisis.

I'm as anxious as a turkey in December.

Stress is when you take tomorrow to bed with you tonight.

Even the trivial seems urgent.

The stressed-out sit on tenterhooks.

Human nature is foolishly fearful, but easily reassured.

The fret set.

Stress is the realisation that you are not in control.

An intelligent man worries about things an idiot doesn't even know about.

The things we worry about most are the least likely to happen.

Don't worry, be happy.

Stress is merely the anxious consideration of overwhelming problems.

Stress is a form of suffering caused by thinking too much.

Apprehension has no limits.

The biggest worry won't fix the smallest problem.

Stress is like opening an umbrella in sunshine, just in case it rains.

Never trouble trouble until trouble troubles you.

Stress is the interest we pay before we even know if we owe anything.

Stress is a treadmill that makes you sweat for nothing.

Never eat jelly. It's more nervous than you are.

Blessed is he who is too busy to worry during the day and too tired to worry at night.

Stress is nature's way of keeping you on your toes.

A poorly extinguished fire is soon re-ignited.

The bow too tensely strung snaps easily.

Temptation

When temptation knocks, imagination answers the door.

Maybe next time.

If you get the urge, fight it.

No-one ever broke a speed record running away from temptation.

If you could resist it, you didn't really want it anyway.

A good resolution is a futile attempt to interfere with nature's gift of temptation.

Temptation is the art of presenting the right inducement at the right time.

An open door can tempt a saint.

Without the added spice of guilt, temptation cannot be fully savoured.

The only way to get rid of temptation is to give in to it.

It's all Eve's fault.

If you resist temptation today, you may not get another shot at it tomorrow.

Lead me not into temptation, it's more fun finding it on my own.

From a certain age onwards, resisting temptation no longer takes strength.

The temptation you resisted is the pleasure you missed out on.

Everything is a temptation to a man who fears temptation.

Virtue is so praiseworthy that rogues practice it from self-interest.

Pleasure is a sin, but what a pleasure sin is.

Temptation laughs at those who take it seriously.

She gave me of the tree, and I did eat. Apples to you too.

Subdue your appetite, and you've conquered human nature.

Freezing weather can tempt an honest man to steal kindling.

What you resist becomes a virtue you boast of, and everyone hates a self-righteous ass.

I can resist anything except temptation.

It's good to have no vices, but it's terrible to be without temptation.

Virtue is insufficient temptation.

It takes courage to give in, any fool can resist.

When temptation constantly saunters by, just wait for it to pass.

Virtuous people resist temptation, but it makes them unbearably self-righteous.

The best protection against temptation is cowardice.

The mind is tempted, not the body. So, if there is no intention, there can be no blame.

If you eat with the devil, use a long spoon.

I generally resist temptation, unless I can't resist it.

The right temptation can overcome a saint.

Temptation should be left to the congenitally sinful, who know when to resist and when to concede.

We want what is forbidden.

We're all honest until something we can't resist tempts us.

I say no weekly, weakly.

Not everyone is lucky enough to find another outlet for his envy.

The one you knock back is the one you don't get.

I can't boast about resisting my greatest temptation, because my wife would kill me.

Eve didn't want the apple for the apple's sake, but because it was forbidden.

Tempt fate. Go on, I dare you.

There is a charm about the forbidden that makes it unspeakably desirable.

Don't pack dry wood too close to the fire.

Existence

Life

You'll never get out of it alive.

Life isn't a cabaret, it's a bloody circus.

How do you know how to play when the rules keep changing?

One day you're the dog, the next day you're the tree.

Life is an incurable disease that will eventually kill you.

If life is a joke, who are we amusing?

The great secret of life is that there is no great secret of life.

There is no sensible answer, because the question doesn't make any sense.

Life isn't about having good cards, it's about playing a poor hand well.

Life is ten percent what you make it, and ninety percent how you take it.

Life is a tragedy for those who feel, and a comedy for those who think.

If life is a joke, death is the punch line.

Between the wish and the real thing, life lies in wait.

Only man sees his existence as a problem he has to solve.

Life is like licking honey off barbed wire.

Every life has its own excuse for being.

In time, we all become the same, nothing.

When you've tried your best and still didn't win, that's life.

It's life alright, but not as we know it.

Shit happens.

Life is the perpetual surprise of existence.

Life is the curiosity by which we test the limits of society.

To live is to be divinely aware.

Everyone wants to live a long time, but no-one wants to be old.

The most important things in life aren't things.

Life isn't one thing after another, it's the same old thing again and again.

Life is short, live it up.

Live simply so that others might simply live.

Life is that irritating interval between sleeps.

In spite of the cost of living, life is still popular.

Life's greatest lesson is that even fools are sometimes right.

When you put your best foot forward and someone steps on it, that's life.

Mere survival is an affliction.

May you live as long as you want, and never want as long as you live.

Some people go through life running away from something that isn't chasing them.

The tragedy of life is what dies inside as we live.

Life is the period between the illusion of immortality and the reality of death.

When you're so high on life that you think you can fly, gravity proves an unforgiving foe.

Life allows us to yearn, but gives us what it thinks we deserve.

The best things in life are free, plus tax of course.

The mystery of life is in the eye of the beholder.

There are more toll roads than freeways on the road to life.

You only make yourself unhappy if you try to adapt society to suit you.

Death

Even when the play has been a happy one, the ending is tragic.

People are dying to get into that cemetery in the dead centre of the city.

If I can survive death, I can survive anything.

May you be in heaven for thirty years before the devil finds out you're dead.

By and by God caught his eye.

Death is the ultimate horror of life.

Death surprises us in the midst of our plans for the future.

Immortality is a fate worse than death.

I'm not afraid to die, I just don't want to be there when it happens.

If my husband was still alive, he would have been dead a year today.

Those who welcome death have only tried it from the ears up.

Just when I finally got it all organised, life is over.

Because I could not stop for Death, he kindly stopped for me.

I've never wished anyone dead, but there are some obituaries I've read with pleasure.

Don't die until you're dead.

If you liked life on earth, you're going to love heaven.

Since we have to speak well of the dead, knock them while they're alive.

I want to die peacefully in my sleep like my father, not screaming in terror like his passengers.

I postpone death by living.

When the oil is exhausted, the lamp goes out.

Death pays all debts.

She was devastated when he died. There she is, in the black tennis dress.

It's not the length of the play that matters, it's the quality of the script.

Where there's a will, I want to be in it.

Nature is honest, people embalm their dead.

The prerequisite for immortality is death.

A rich distant relative's death is a lucky stroke.

A posthumous work is created by someone after they're dead.

Death is perpetual retirement without pay.

Obituary is the last write.

Death is nature's way of telling you to slow down.

Death has a thousand doors to let out life.

You leave behind what you have, and take with you what you are.

He would be enormously improved by death.

Yesterday was the last day of your life.

Death is not as bad as the fear of dying.

A headstone remembers what has become dust.

Your failure to take out life insurance ensures it will be a sad day for your relatives.

Death is the absence of presence.

Without life, death would not be possible.

Nothing improves character as much as an obituary does.

A poor man's roast and a rich man's death can be smelled from afar.

Live well, leave little.

Spend it yourself, don't let the funeral directors and lawyers have it.

Happiness

Happiness is an inside job.

Happiness comes in through the door you forgot to close.

I want life, liberty and a Porsche in which to pursue happiness.

You wouldn't be normal if you smiled all the time, you'd be a game show host.

Happiness is contagious. Spread it.

Happiness is good health and a bad memory.

Money can't buy happiness, but it lets you enjoy a pleasant sort of misery.

Start every day with a smile, just to get it over and done with.

So you're not happy, is that anything to cry about?

Happiness is not enough, I want paradise.

I'm too happy, what am I doing right?

If you can't be happy with what you have, be grateful for what you escaped.

It's bitter to see happiness through another's eyes.

A dog wags its tail with it's heart.

When happiness gets into your system, it breaks out all over your face.

Happiness is a journey, not a destination.

It is bitter to see happiness through another's eyes.

Happiness is always finding a new goal to strive for.

Happiness is where you find it, not where you look for it.

It's the friendship you find along the way.

Money may not buy happiness, but it does attract interesting companions.

As soon as you ask yourself whether you're happy, you cease to be.

How can you expect someone else to make you happy when you can't even do it yourself?

The happiest people have no history.

Happiness is a well-kept conscience.

Live each day as if it was the first day of your honeymoon or the last day of your holiday.

Most people confuse excitement with happiness, and wonder why it doesn't last..

What difference will a change of scenery make if you're miserable anyway?

Happiness is halfway between too much and too little.

Misery spreads happiness everywhere it doesn't go.

Some people have a highly developed instinct for being unhappy.

When we're happy, time flies. When we're not, it hobbles along on crutches.

I am happy because I think I am.

Who is content with little possesses much.

Happiness is blue skies and green lights all the way.

If you can't be content here, how will you find happiness there?

Happiness is a pleasant sensation arising from the misery of others.

Our happiest days are always in the past.

Happiness is the brief period between periods of unhappiness.

The rich think the poor are happy, the poor think the rich are happy.

If you stood still and stopped pursuing happiness, it would catch up with you.

Happiness is a by-product of achievement.

To be satisfied with what you have is happiness.

It's the fulfilment of the soul through the body.

Sorrow

My pain is not diminished by your anguish.

To see the road ahead clearly, you have to give your tears time to dry.

If only you were here right now to upset me again.

Friendship doubles our joy and halves our grief.

Grief is a burden that cannot be shared, everyone has to carry his own.

Tragedy is the gift that keeps on giving.

I think, therefore I am depressed.

Pain is inevitable, suffering is optional.

This too shall pass.

Pain is gain.

Elaborate funerals are for the vanity of the living and not the glory of the dead.

The chief mourner doesn't always attend the funeral.

Perhaps the dead are free, but the living remain and bleed for them.

Never feel guilty about surviving, those who are gone live on in the hearts of we who loved them.

The pain of sorrow is the evidence of life.

Oh, for the sound of that beloved voice which is silent.

No-one mourns more ostentatiously than those who feel no grief.

Time heals wounds.

While sorrow is fresh, all attempts to divert it cause anger.

Grief can take care of itself, but joy needs to be shared.

He was nothing to the world, but to me he was everything.

Sorrow isn't contagious, although many people act as though it was.

Don't waste fresh tears on old grief.

You have to have known sorrow to be able to appreciate happiness.

Idleness increases grief.

Those who have never experienced sorrow cannot sympathise with those who have.

There is no remedy for grief that is concealed.

The soul would have no rainbow, had the eye no tears.

Grief sharpens understanding and softens the heart.

When anything dies, something mourns.

Grief has its own language.

Sometimes sorrow grows on a branch too weak to bear it.

Two in distress diminishes sorrow.

Time drags for those who grieve.

Sorrow travels uphill, it's difficult to bear but impossible to maintain in the long run.

There is no pain in the memory of a past sorrow.

The memory of a past sorrow makes your present joy so much sweeter.

If you have a broken heart, how can sweet words possibly fix it?

If you don't know what to say, a hug speaks volumes.

Do not look back in anger, or forward in fear, but look around in awareness.

Some people cultivate an air of what they assume is fashionable unhappiness.

Long term sorrow is the result of too much introspection.

True grief shies away from publicity.

The ceremonious air of doom and gloom makes death a hideous show.

Failure

Apathy

So much routine, so little reason.

There's no point tapping your feet if you can't hear the music.

Motion, promotion, demotion, death.

Apathy is having a ten year-old child you haven't named yet.

I couldn't care less about apathy.

Apathy is when you don't care whether that little black thing in your dessert is a fly or a raison.

Shame on the soul, the body perseveres.

Same shit, different day.

All this time I thought I was learning how to live, but in fact I was preparing to die.

Of course I don't hate you, but I'm still going to eat you.

I care for nobody and nobody cares for me.

So what if apathy is the biggest problem facing society today.

Eat right, live clean, exercise. Die anyway.

Hate is not the opposite of love, apathy is.

It's insulting to beauty not to see it.

Apathy is when you die before you're dead.

I have a care factor of zero and it's still dropping.

To save a man's life against his will is the same as killing him.

And how much will you be donating to the Indian Relief Fund, Mrs. Custer?

There's no point in singing to a deaf man.

The sun will rise and set without my help.

The opportunity I missed today may present itself again tomorrow, but if it doesn't, who cares?

If practice makes perfect, but nobody is perfect, why practice?

Those who don't care about life are already three quarters dead.

Apathy is the ability to pass on gossip without embroidering on it.

I'm not apathetic, I just don't give a damn.

If it wasn't for physics, I'd be unstoppable.

Some people are dead long before they die.

The greatest menace is inertia.

Win or lose, I'll be okay.

Since the house next door is on fire anyway, let's roast marshmallows.

Life is the interim between birth and death.

Nothing really matters except for a few things, and they don't matter very much.

Apathy is worse than sorrow, because it shows where sorrow once lived.

It is sad to die, but it's worse never to have lived.

The essence of inhumanity is indifference.

What's the use of running if you have nowhere to go?

So what? Who cares?

The rich would not be apathetic about the poor if they had to see them every day.

Due to lack of interest, tomorrow has been cancelled.

If you have never despaired, how can you hope?

Apart from that, Mrs. Lincoln, how did you enjoy the play?

Failure

Show me a good loser and I'll show you a loser.

A successful man is a failure who persisted until he got it right.

He who lies on the ground cannot fall down, but he will be trod on by he who has some get up and go.

I am thinking positively, I'm positive I'm going to fail.

If at first you don't succeed, maybe you ought to settle for failure.

Things only go right so that they can ultimately go wrong.

He's a self made man and you can't help wondering who interrupted him.

Defeat is when you've struggled to the top of the ladder, only to find it's leaning against the wrong wall.

I refuse to try, in case I make the wrong mistake.

The only thing achieved without effort is failure.

It's better to lose with honour than to win by cheating, but only if your situation is already hopeless.

I had a ticket to the good life, but I missed the boat.

Defeat is a temporary situation, giving up is what makes it permanent.

I started out with nothing and I'm back where I started.

I know I'm going the wrong way, so it's just as well I'm going so slow.

He's utterly unspoiled by all his great failures.

Just because I don't have the solution, doesn't mean I can't admire the problem.

Nothing fails like success.

When the water is over your head, it doesn't matter how deep it is.

Don't be discouraged by defeat, it's merely a fresh stimulus to do better.

Most failures are good at making excuses.

To decide not to decide is a decision. To fail to decide to defer, is failure.

Celebrate the victory, analyse the defeat.

At twenty he knew nothing, at forty he'd done nothing, and at sixty he was nothing.

Failure makes us intolerant of success.

The worst type of failure is the failure to try again.

Your salary gets docked while you're waiting for your ship to come in.

Judging by the silence, he's just told a joke.

You never know where bottom is until you reach it.

Failure to prepare is preparing to fail.

He's destined to go far, and the sooner the better.

I started out with nothing and I still have everything I started with.

Don't follow the path, strike your own trail.

He waited so long for his ship to come in that the wharf collapsed.

He's not a quitter, he always gets fired.

The only advantage of going to her party is that you know you'll get home early. Winning may not be everything, but losing isn't anything.

What was the name of the fourth man to walk on the moon?

Also-ran is the name of all the horses that didn't win.

You can observe a lot just by watching.

Not all those who wander are lost.

You can run with the big dogs, or sit on the porch and bark.

Losing is a lot of not much.

Rust wastes more than use.

Incompetence

Leave it for tomorrow, you've made enough mistakes for today.

Whatever he's got, he hasn't got enough of it.

If you can't learn from your mistakes, don't bother making any.

The person who can't dance always accuses the band of playing out of tune.

It's hard to soar like an eagle when you work with turkeys.

Asking stupid questions is better than correcting stupid mistakes.

It's better to know some of the questions than all of the answers.

If something goes wrong, make it look as though it was intentional.

A clever man still makes mistakes, but a fool persists in his.

You don't need a cannon to kill a spider.

It's not enough to have good aim if you've run out of ammunition.

I might have won beauty competitions, if I wasn't so damn ugly.

An excuse is an apology offered for failure to complete a task.

Perfect aim is useless if you forget to load.

Never clap too loudly in a condemned building.

A single tree can't make a forest.

If you can't do what you'd like to do, do what you can do.

If we try, we err.

Errors by great men are more memorable because they produce more than the truths of insignificant men.

If at first you don't succeed, destroy all evidence that you ever tried.

What you think you see isn't necessarily what you'll get.

If humanity profits from its mistakes, then we should have a glorious future ahead of us.

Whatever you've got, get rid of it.

A bad workman always blames his tools.

Two wrongs are only the beginning.

You can complain about the tune, but don't attack the monkey if the organ grinder is present.

Mistakes are nature's way of telling us the current thinking is incomplete.

You can't clap with one hand.

When you're not a self-starter, the world is filled with cranks.

The difference in lifestyle lies between capability and performance.

I took an IQ test and the result came back negative.

If you won't try, you've already lost.

Sink or swim.

You can make excuses for him, but not for those who encouraged him.

When the boss does it, it's called delegating.

In order to be, I must participate.

To err is human, to blame it on others even more so.

A bad workman never gets a good tool.

Error is the war between instinct and reason.

The person who owns up is more honest than the person who claims they don't make mistakes.

If it wasn't for her voice, she could have been a famous singer.

It's a bad bridge that doesn't span the river.

Laziness

It's not missing a deadline that I hate so much, it's the shouting that accompanies it.

To hell with deadlines, the slower you work, the fewer mistakes you make.

If you go slow for long enough, you'll be in the lead again.

Efficiency is intelligent laziness.

Lazy people have as much initiative as an echo.

Indecision is the key to flexibility.

The sooner you fall behind, the more time you have to catch up.

An excuse means someone respects you too much to simply ignore you.

Yes, I know I procrastinate, and I'll deal with it sooner or later.

If I was indispensable, I couldn't be promoted.

Many hands want light work.

Problems that go away by themselves, come back by themselves.

Much might have been done, sooner.

Never put off till tomorrow what you can avoid altogether.

I was afraid of doing too much, and I ended up doing too little.

The lazier a man is, the more he intends to do tomorrow.

Killing time murders opportunities.

Laziness is often mistaken for patience.

I'm not satisfied, but I'm too lazy to kick up a fuss.

I would have done it if you hadn't nagged me about it.

The devil finds work for idle hands.

Trying times are a good time to quit trying.

Never do today what you can put off until tomorrow.

A little activity sits on a big butt.

Low Incomes live on Easy Street.

What doesn't flow soon becomes stagnant.

Use it before you lose it.

Laziness is a luxury few can afford.

The longer it is deferred, the more difficult it becomes.

He has to work up the energy to take a nap.

Nothing would ever be attempted if every single obstacle had to be overcome first.

Laziness is a warm coat, but it doesn't suit all seasons.

A lazy man is never lucky.

Some sit and wait, and some just sit.

What you see is not necessarily what you get.

If we profit from our mistakes, how come we aren't all millionaires?

No-one is more precise at measuring his free time than the man whose time is all free.

The quality of life can't be measured by its lack of activity.

Nature is motion.

Lazy people are always too busy to relax.

If you just fiddle around, you'll never lead the band.

Laziness loses its sweetness when it becomes the norm.

Some people do nothing, but they do it well.

If you're too lazy to clean your windows, the world outside looks hazy.

Laziness is being inactive without actually relaxing.

Laziness travels so slowly that poverty overtakes it.

Making mistakes is a sign of activity.

Family

Home

Home is where you go when you get tired of being nice to people.

Men build houses, women make homes.

We live in a mansion overlooking the rent.

Every bird likes it's own nest best.

The family's place in society marks the level of civilization.

A man's home is his wife's castle.

If you're looking for trouble, there's no place like home.

Home is where your stuff is.

Work is where husbands go to escape from home.

You make beds and wash dishes and a few months later you have to start from scratch and do it all over again.

The essence of a home lies in its permanence.

Meals used to be thought out, now they're thawed out.

You can't fool the mother, she really does have eyes in the back of her head.

Happiness is a big family, who live very far away.

Family reunions are the greatest justification for birth control.

Home is a woman's workhouse.

There is no such thing as *fun for the whole family.*

Home is where you kick off your new shoes and put on your old manners.

I am a daughter in my mother's home, but a mistress in my own.

Home is where you grew up.

People who have glass doors might as well answer the doorbell.

We have no children, except me.

Home is where men go when the pubs shut.

Alcoholism is not a spectator sport, all the family participate.

To move three times is as traumatic as a fire.

Blood is thicker than water, but so is grease.

Home is where a housewife stays when the car is in for repairs.

Only condemn nepotism if the relatives don't work.

Children may tear up a house, but they never break up a home.

Parental servitude.

You can choose your friends, but you're stuck with your family.

Home is where you can scratch if it itches.

Fathers are blind to their daughter's faults.

A kitten is a tiger in his own home.

The minute they heard I had been kidnapped, they rented out my room.

A home is where your family is.

Empty nest, happy home.

Some are imprisoned and some are housed in homes.

Home is where the television set is better adjusted than the family.

A house is built with walls and beams, a home is built with love and dreams.

Everyone knows how to raise children until they have their own.

Home is that place we go to when we leave the garage.

Happy homes are built on tolerance.

Fathers can't help competing with their sons.

Babies

Infants are to infancy what adults are to adultery.

Babies are such a nice way to start people.

Of course it's a boy or a girl. What else would it be?

Defenceless little babies have parents totally at their command.

Congratulations, we all knew you had it in you.

If you think it's so easy to take candy from a baby, try it.

You spend the first year waiting for them to walk and talk, and the next twenty years waiting for them to sit down and shut up.

I hate babies. They look so frighteningly human.

The birth of a baby is a vote of confidence in the future.

We don't know what the baby's name is yet, because we still can't understand a word he says.

The spitting image of his father takes on a whole new meaning when feeding a baby.

When a baby cries, you've got a choice of two openings.

I can't believe that out of ten million sperm, you were the quickest.

Life is tough enough without having to kick your way out.

I was a war baby, my folks took one look at me and they started fighting.

A playpen is useful when a toddler throws tantrums. When the toddler calms down, the parent climbs out.

Born free? I don't think so.

The last people on earth who should have children are parents.

Caring for a baby has to be learned from the bottom up.

A baby is a sample of humanity.

Having a baby is like pulling your bottom lip up over your head.

Insomnia is a contagious disease passed from babies to mothers.

His mother should have thrown him away and kept the stork.

People who say they slept like a baby obviously don't have one.

I was born there because I thought it was important to be near my mother.

They named me Sue, after the verb.

Childbirth is like trying to pull your car out through its exhaust pipe.

A baby is a loud voice at one end and no sense of responsibility at the other.

We named him Bill because he was born on the first of the month.

Babies shut their eyes so often just to lull parents into a false sense of security.

With the first baby, you sterilise the dummy. With the second baby, you tell the dog to *fetch* the dummy.

If you didn't eat it, how come it's in your stomach?

Babies range from rug rats to ankle biters.

As if childbirth wasn't bad enough, then you're expected to keep it.

Once upon a time, and a very good time it was, day care centres were called homes.

Babies leak from both ends.

A baby is God's opinion that the world should go on.

Here we have a baby, an object consisting of a bald head, a smelly rear end, and a pair of lungs.

They're especially good with sweet and sour sauce, or stewed.

This is what they meant when they said, *May all your troubles be little ones.*

A shortcut is the distance between a baby and anything breakable.

Boys have sex, girls have babies.

Children

There's nothing thirstier than a child who's just gone to bed.

What a child's opinion lacks in kindness, it makes up for in clarity.

You can tell, just by looking at a child, what sort of past he's going to have.

A sweater is something a child puts on when his mother gets cold.

Explain the concept of death carefully, to ensure your threats are more effective.

A child that's loved has many names.

Too noisy and they punish you, too quiet and they think you're sick.

Give the neighbours' children an inch, and they'll take a yard.

I was the kind of child my mother told me not to play with.

The secret of dealing successfully with a child is not to be its parent.

When a child lives with approval, he learns to like himself.

An alarm clock is an instrument used to wake people who don't have small children.

A boy is an appetite, surrounded by noise with dirt on it.

Sometimes I look at my children and wonder why I never considered abortion.

Don't limit your child to your own experience, because he was born in a different time.

My mother loved children. She would have given anything for me to have been one.

Never hit a child in the face, there's a place for everything.

I have the heart of a child, which I keep in a jar on my desk.

Every mother in the world owns the most perfect child.

Some praise the child for the mother's sake.

Ask the young. They know everything.

Raising children is an exercise in heir-conditioning.

A child remains a child until there is another child.

Children need love, especially those who least deserve it.

We would have been divorced years ago, but neither of us wanted them.

The only thing a child shares willingly is his mother's age.

What's precious to children has no price, only value.

The best time to tackle a little problem is before it grows up.

They may not always listen, but they imitate well.

I love a crying child, because someone always comes to fetch him.

Regeneration.

A child is never more willing to run an errand than he is at bedtime.

Never have more children than you have car windows.

Children should have pets, but only until the pets start having children.

When will children ever learn that *no* is a complete sentence?

Children never put off until tomorrow what can keep them out of bed tonight.

Praise the child and you make love to the mother.

Beat your children once a day, if you don't know why, they do.

It's usually that little devil at school who starts the fights with your little angel.

Great oaks grow from little acorns.

How we treat our children is how they will treat their children.

The child survives in the adult.

Children should be seen and not had.

You can train a child until he's ten, but thereafter you merely influence him.

There's nothing more affectionate than a child with sticky fingers.

All children are essentially criminal.

Parents

Only a mother knows the joy of having dinner with two other people who don't kick each other under the table.

It's not easy being a mother. If it were, fathers would do it.

Parents are couples who practised the Rhythm Method.

The children got their brains from their mother. Their father still has his.

Children produce parents.

Child psychology is what children use to manage their parents with.

Parents are big kids acting like adults so that little kids don't get frightened.

If you give in often enough, you end up giving up.

No wonder parents can't communicate with their teenagers, the music is too loud.

Never raise your hand to your children. It leaves your middle unprotected.

No-one understands the concept of being driven insane better than a parent.

The parents of reasonable children have children with reasonable parents.

The best time to put the children to bed is while you still have the strength.

If you want a child's undivided attention, whisper.

Some parents are distant relatives.

Alligators and rats have the right idea, they eat their young.

Some praise the child for the mother's sake.

Happy are those who are happy with their children.

You can raise them or let them down.

A rich child often sits on a poor mother's lap.

When you do too much for them, they do nothing for themselves.

When you're constantly disciplining children, it doesn't take long before you begin to sound like one.

May my children have wealthy parents.

A babysitter is someone you pay to watch your children as they do whatever they want.

I used to have all these theories about raising children, now I have all these children and no theories.

Next year two million children will become teenagers, and four million parents will turn pale.

We taught our children the value of money, but not the concept of inflation.

Parents are people who lie awake at night wondering whether their daughter's new dreamboat is going to turn into their worst nightmare.

The average teenager still has all the problems his parents outgrew.

You know you've lost control when you're the one who goes to your room.

Children are a pain in the neck when they're around, and an ache in the heart when they're not.

Before we had children, I went home to rest. Now I go to work to have a rest.

If you want something done, forbid the kids from doing it.

The accent is on youth and the stress is on parents.

If the human body evolved over millions of years, why do mothers still only have two arms?

Shopping with children should be made an Olympic event.

A silly question is one a parent can't answer.

You have to give parents credit, they really know how to obey their children.

Despite our best efforts to raise our children decently, they still act like us.

Grandparents

If Mum says no, ask Grandma.

Baby clothes are what keep grannies warm in their old age.

I don't mind being a grandfather, but I hate sleeping with a grandmother.

Nothing enhances a child's abilities like a grandparent.

Grandparents are so simple that a child can operate them.

No, you haven't shown me the photographs of your grandchildren, and I'm so grateful.

Grandchildren are God's reward for resisting the temptation to kill your own kids when they misbehaved.

A grandparent's pleasures are the parents' duties.

Grandparents have all the time in the world for fun and games now, something they never had when their own children were growing up.

The reason that grandparents and grandchildren get along so well is that they have a common enemy.

If I'd known how much fun grandchildren were, I'd have skipped having children of my own.

A grandmother is someone who puts you to bed when she's tired.

They need your presence far more than they need your presents.

Grandma knows best, but no-one ever listens.

A grandparent is someone who no longer cares whether they're good parents or not, as long as the kids are happy.

Grandparents bore teenagers and babysit little children.

The food at Grandma's is always better than the stuff at home.

Grandparents are the bones upon which grandchildren cut their teeth.

Have children while your parents are still young enough to look after them.

Just when she's ready for a rest, along came the grandchildren.

When the going gets tough, the tough go to Grandma.

Grandparents are never child proof.

Slow down, grandparents crossing.

Grandchildren get the most out of middle age.

We don't have to discipline our grandchildren. That's the parents' job.

Finally the house is tidy, and along come the grandchildren.

Grandparents retire to the coast just to escape being unpaid babysitters.

A grandparent overlooks behaviour in grandchildren that would have been unforgivable in their own children.

Being a grandmother is great, but I hate living with a pensioner.

Grandchildren are nature's way of compensating us for growing old.

A mother doesn't notice the terrible things her children do because she's so entranced with the wonderful things her grandchildren do.

The purpose of grandchildren is to teach parents what has happened in the world since our own children grew up.

The best part of being a grandparent is the promotion from executioner to observer.

By the time your own children are old enough to keep the house tidy, their children are messing it up.

Grandparents remind grandchildren of incidents parents would rather forget.

If the baby is a perfect little angel all the time, chances are you're the grandmother.

You start to show your age as soon as the baby pictures start doing the rounds.

Government

Bureaucrats

Hell hath no fury like a bureaucrat scorned.

Nothing to do all day except be rude to taxpayers.

Nothing pleases a small mind more than the opportunity to crack the whip.

Policy is the shield I hide behind.

I only opened up so that I could tell you we're closed.

Civil servants deserve to be treated like human beings because, deep down, they are.

God helps those who help themselves, and those caught helping themselves.

A bureaucracy has more patience than you can ever imagine having.

A legend is his own lunchtime.

All bureaucrats are indistinguishable from their predecessors.

Parliament is an immense monument to man's subservience to the desk.

It takes a bureaucracy to fight a bureaucracy.

We don't care. We don't have to.

So little horse sense, so much horse shit.

The persistence of bureaucrats varies inversely with the importance of the matter on which they are persisting.

Corruption is greed with its sleeves rolled up.

Bureaucracy is a giant organisation which is managed by midgets.

Once a misfit resigns, another will be recruited.

Of course I have the answers, you're just not asking the right questions.

There are too many chiefs and not enough Indians.

I know more about economics than my examiners.

Power corrupts. Absolute power constitutes a bureaucracy.

When something goes wrong, just pass the blame on down the line until either the music stops, or the caller hangs up.

The greater the funding, the longer it takes to uncover the corruption.

Bigger isn't better.

When in doubt, delegate.

Once he gets home, he ceases to be the boss.

Enlarging departments isn't the solution. It's the problem.

It's a distant process for which its exponents feel no personal responsibility.

Public office is the last refuge of the incompetent.

He poses as the servant, but knows he is the master.

He makes copies of all his obsolete files before he shreds them.

They've overcome gravity, but the paperwork is overwhelming.

The civil servants are uncivil.

Memorandums are written not to inform the reader, but to protect the writer.

Bureaucracy creates the illusion of progress by constantly reorganising, just when little bureaucrats are beginning to learn their jobs.

When in trouble, delegate.

Bureaucrats shoot the bull, pass the buck and roll out kilometres of red tape.

If a bureaucrat hangs around long enough, he ends up somewhere.

Bureaucrats are hired only if they pass a test to establish their lack of initiative.

So much time and money is spent on allotting blame that the funds run out before the problem is rectified.

Government

Somewhere along the line they stopped doing things for us, and started doing them to us.

They govern best who govern least.

We will either stamp out corruption, or allow the public to participate in it.

A dead fish always stinks from the head downwards.

Never believe rumours until they've been officially denied.

We're over-governed and underprivileged because we took freedom for granted.

They privatised the electricity commission, and kept us in the dark.

If they take credit for the rain, we're entitled to blame them for the drought.

The one-man one-vote concept died the instant they began to play around with electoral boundaries.

Socialism begins as creeping communism and ends as galloping over reaction.

ASIO produces more history than it consumes locally.

If this is what it's like when they're on our side, thank heavens they're not against us.

Most of our plans are merely inaccurate predictions.

We only demand freedom after we are deprived of power.

The problem with political jokes is that they now run the country.

Everybody makes mistakes. That's why we keep having elections.

Government is a matter of survival of the best connected.

A subsidy is when the government gives you some of your own money back.

Communism is socialism with official enforcers.

If voting could really change anything, the government wouldn't allow it.

We get the government we deserve.

The only government enterprise that ever made money was the mint.

A democracy is where everyone has an equal right to feel superior.

The mystery of government is not in knowing how it works, but in how to stop it.

The government bans firecrackers, but pays arms dealers to manufacture bombs.

They take from those who work and give it to those who don't.

A democracy is a country where it's safe to be unpopular.

The king's favour is no inheritance.

Capitalism is survival of the fattest.

The golden rule is that those with gold rule.

Fascism is capitalism in decay.

No country has ever been starved into democracy.

A decent government is a blessing, but what nation has ever had it?

I used to believe they wouldn't be in power if they didn't know what they were doing.

You can't fool all the people all the time, which is why we have cover ups.

A democracy is where you can say what you think, even if you can't think for yourself.

For every action, there is an equal and opposite government programme working against it.

Capitalism offers an unequal share of wealth with the powerful, and socialism offers an equal share of wealth for those in power.

To be pinko, or better dead than red, that is the question.

Communism works best where it isn't needed, and worst where they already have it.

Isn't it amazing how much they spend on policies they swear they're not thinking of implementing?

Income Tax

The Lord giveth and the government taketh away.

So much tax, so little benefit.

The difference between cheating the taxman and cheating on your wife is that if you're caught, the taxman wants you more than ever.

Put your money where your mouth is, and kiss it goodbye.

Behind every successful man stands an impatient taxman.

Tax is where supply exceeds production, and the government just keeps increasing demand.

Income tax is capital punishment.

Money is the root of all taxes.

With the tax you pay during your lifetime, you'd think the government would have the decency to pay for the funeral.

A lottery is a tax on people who don't understand statistics.

Income tax is the government's bite out of your income.

A dollar saved is a dollar taxed.

Nothing makes a man more modest about his earnings than an income tax return.

If only they could price themselves out of the market.

Public money doesn't seem to belong to anyone, that's why it's so easy for them to throw it around.

Higher income tax is the reward you get for working harder.

Income tax is the government's way of suppressing the masses without resorting to violence.

We need watchdogs to protect us from the mongrels.

You may not know when you're well off, but the government does.

Soon we'll be better off with the deduction instead of the pay.

The road to parliament is paved with taxes.

It's more difficult to fill out your income tax return than it is to earn the income you're taxed on.

We are a nation of untold wealth.

How come there's always enough for foreign aid, but not for local aid?

If democracy is a free country, how come we pay so much tax?

Children may be deductible, but they're still taxing.

The world is made up of givers and takers, and the takers live better.

We all work for the government, one way or another.

Whenever hidden taxes are discovered, they're immediately suspended, but only until a better hiding place can be found.

Untold wealth is undisclosed income.

They deduct tax from your salary and charge you to bank it What you buy with it includes tax and they wonder why you lie about it.

Air is still free. It's where you stand to breathe it that's taxed.

Nothing tests your powers of deduction like an income tax return.

If you could buy happiness, the government would put a perks tax on it.

We used to live within our incomes, and the government lived without ours.

The more they give us, the more it costs us.

Taxes travel uphill, but services are going downhill fast.

They tax you on foresight and penalise you for your oversights.

Politicians

When politicians run, taxpayers sweat.

A statesman is a dead politician. This country needs more statesmen.

If they can't recognise their own speakers in parliament, how can they run the country?

The politician's dance: one step forward, two steps back, and the famous side step.

John Howard has all the charisma of a speed bump, but that speed bump is Kim Beasley's mountain.

There is no such thing as a cheap politician.

The word politics is derived from *poli* meaning many, and *tics,* which are blood sucking parasites.

Every taxpayer has a politician on his payroll.

How can anyone ridicule miracles, yet believe in election promises?

Politics is a part-time occupation which has been exaggerated into a full-time part-time profession.

Don't vote, it only encourages the bastards.

The reason for the gap in elections is to give voters time to regain their faith in politicians.

Politics is the art of getting votes from the poor and campaign funds from the rich, by promising to protect each from the other.

If John Howard is the answer, it must have been a stupid question.

Don't vote for the best candidate. Vote for the one who'll do the least harm.

You don't have to fool all the people all the time, just long enough to be elected.

There are hundreds of honest politicians, but unfortunately they're all dead.

He found out which way the crowd was headed, and followed them in front.

Never judge presidential timber by its bark.

If he's having an affair, we've misjudged him. We thought he only screwed the country.

Make your Member of Parliament work. Don't vote him in again.

The opposition never has to think, they only have to take the opposite viewpoint.

They are often wrong, but never in doubt.

A politician finds out where the people are going so that he can lead them.

It takes a lot of money just to lose an election.

Considering all the candidates, aren't we lucky only one can be elected?

An honest politician is one who, when he has been bought, stays bought.

Being politically correct means perpetually having to say you're sorry.

Even Napolean had his Watergate.

Every clarification breeds a new question.

Politicians rise above their principles.

If we were cannibals, politicians would promise us missionaries for dinner.

A politician is someone who has both feet planted firmly on either side of an issue.

His best asset is his bad memory.

The difference between a pothole and a politician is that most people would swerve to avoid the pothole.

A politician's staff devote weeks to preparing his impromptu speeches.

Politicians promise to build bridges even when there is no river.

Power only retreats in the face of greater power.

To each according to their needs, and they need mansions and chauffeurs.

They confuse free speech with cheap talk.

United Nations

The United Nations has effectively raised the standard of living around the world, but only for its employees.

They speak softly but they send tanks.

Never in the history of the world have so few loused up so much for so many.

Overpaid, overfed, oversexed and over there.

If the ultimate aim is to homogenize society, forget it. What's good for Kenya may be bad for Australia.

The function of the United Nations is to raise suffering to a higher level.

Join the United Nations. Travel to exciting places, meet interesting people, and kill them.

The big five have luxurious cabins, the poor sit on the deck, and all the other nations row the boat.

Foreign aid buys food, for armies.

Join the United Nations and invade the country of your choice in comfort.

The United Nations operates on taxes from poor people in rich countries for the benefit of rich people in poor countries.

The big five make the poor perform for peanuts, and all the other nations provide the peanuts.

Your country's contribution may well buy the bullet that kills your son overseas.

Their ultimate aim is to distribute poverty equally throughout the world.

Too many foreign nations are living beyond our means.

Every country gets the government it deserves, until the United Nations decides otherwise.

When elephants fight, the mice underfoot get trampled.

They support amenable dictators, rendering the democratic right impotent.

The end result of foreign aid is war.

They create desolation in the name of peace.

Honesty is the worst foreign policy.

The farmer treats the turkey well, until thanksgiving.

To hell with the UN, why can't we peel our own bananas?

It is a declaration of love, with the promise of a mass marriage.

Aiding and abetting the enemy used to be called treason, now they call it foreign aid.

Diplomats are fine in good weather, but if it rains they drown in a single drop.

The United Nations makes waves and then deserts a sinking ship.

Every day is the International Day of the United Nations Pay Day.

Foreign aid is proof taxpayers pay too much. The government is simply giving it away to strangers.

The lunatics have taken charge of the asylum.

More people die through aid received from the United Nations than are helped by it.

The United Nations have the whole world eating out of their hand.

This is bureaucracy on an international scale.

God cares for people through people, and the United Nations knows exactly what God wants.

If a portion of our taxes is paid to support the United Nations, how come we can't claim them as a dependant?

Foreign aid is like putting a band-aid on a cut throat.

War

He profits most who makes the guns used in the duel.

Soldiers don't fight for principles, but to defend their government's prejudice.

Military intelligence is a contradiction in terms.

You can no more win a war than you can win an earthquake.

They only advocate war as a means of peace.

Men love war because it stops women laughing at them.

Just kill everyone, and let God sort it out.

Don't endanger your lives needlessly until I give you the signal.

Glory in war is a theatrical concept.

Nuclear disarmament is an explosive argument.

We never punish murderers who kill to the sound of trumpets.

There are degrees of loss, but no-one can win a war.

War is like love. It can always find a way.

The real hero is the man who stops the war.

After each war, there is less democracy to save.

War is the ultimate male ego trip.

A nation is only at peace with itself when it is at war with another nation.

They never advocate war except as a means of peace.

Guns and bombs are symbols of human failure.

Take the diplomacy out of war, and it's just another ugly squirmish.

It's not just cruelty that leads men into war. It's excitement.

The tragedy of war is that it uses man's best to do his worst.

War is politics enforced.

Can you trust your prime minister with his finger on your country's trigger?

How good bad music and good reasons sound when we march against an enemy.

Old men declare wars and young men die fighting them.

Laws are silent in time of war.

War never leaves a nation as far forward as it found it.

War crime tribunals incriminate only a select few.

One day they'll give a war and nobody will come.

A war without headquarters is an expedition.

Praise the Lord and pass the ammunition.

In war, truth is always the first casualty.

God is always on the side of the heaviest battalion.

Hi ho, hi ho, it's hand grenades I throw.

He leads his platoon from the rear, so that when they retreat, he will be in front.

An army is a separate nation within the same nation.

The end of the war doesn't bring back the dead.

To die sooner in war, is to suffer less.

There is no such thing as a good war or a bad peace.

War is an escape from the problems of peace.

Soldiers win battles and generals get the credit.

War is the government's solution to overpopulation.

War doesn't prove who was right, only who was stronger.

War is like love. It always finds a way.

Harmony

Charity

I give you charity, you give me fame.

Only the very rich can afford charity dinners for the poor.

Delete the ego, and you castrate the benefactor.

The less that trickles out, the more noise it makes.

No-one does more harm than those who go around doing good.

We make people pay dearly for what we think we gave them.

Charity covers a multitude of sins.

Money is like manure. If you don't spread it around, it just piles up and stinks.

They've taken God off the charity list and put him on the payroll.

You can't help someone up a hill without getting closer to the top yourself.

No-one looks a gift horse in the mouth.

Charity used to be an added bonus, now it's a taxable deduction.

Who would have thought that I could get so rich from catering to the poor?

A good deed never goes unpunished.

I know what I've given you, do you understand what you've received?

The problem with giving till it hurts is that some people are more sensitive than others.

When I hand you a hundred dollar note, it will be the dirtiest one I can find.

We all fight the urge to bite the hand that feeds us.

It's better to give than to lend, and it costs about the same.

I give you money because my time is too expensive.

Charity handicaps the recipient by making him dependent upon it.

A dog won't howl if you throw meatballs at him.

To accept the gift is to be obligated.

There is a sublime form of theft in all giving.

Better to be a hammer than a nail.

You give most when you give of yourself.

When it comes to charity, some people stop at nothing.

The most sincere gift is a portion of yourself.

As cold as charity.

Thank heavens the poor will always be with us, or some of us wouldn't have jobs.

When he gives you much, he owns you.

What you get for free costs too much.

Charity goes toward easing the plight of the poor, but diminishes on the way.

If you have given only money, you haven't given much.

Give appropriately, a pair of boots is of no use to a man with no feet.

He merits no kindness who does a service for his own ends.

Gold isn't worthless just because it is given out of a sense of duty.

A tree feeds off the soil and is tied to it, the sky asks for nothing and is free.

A charity banquet is an expensive but mediocre dinner where you pay to be seen, and if there's anything left over, it goes to the poor.

We, with plenty, ease our conscience by giving to those with nothing.

Cheat on your taxes and you'll be able to give more to charity.

The middle class is too proud to beg but has too much to receive alms.

Charity dinners are plates of food surrounded by appeals for donations.

Courtesy

Courtesy may not be dead, but it definitely isn't using public transport.

I remember courtesy perfectly, but I can't place its face.

Courtesy is contagious. Pray for an epidemic.

You are rude, crude, uncouth, unattractive, and socially unacceptable.

Good manners are the noise you don't make when you're eating soup.

Good manners need the support of good manners in others.

You can't be truly rude before you understand good manners.

Never ask what's cooking in a crematorium.

Behaviour is a mirror in which others see our true image reflected.

Keep practicing, good manners will probably become fashionable again.

Manners are not worth much in themselves, but they add value to everything else.

Our conduct is determined by our upbringing.

Good manners are made up of many petty little sacrifices.

Single sided courtesy doesn't last long.

Being polite to your wife only makes her sure you've been up to no good.

He is the very pineapple of politeness.

Good manners is the ability to yawn with your mouth closed.

A lady never flattens a gentleman without extreme provocation.

Politeness is the chief sign of culture.

Good manners are the rituals that separate the coarse from the refined.

If you want courteous and efficient service, help yourself.

Nothing is more vulgar than haste.

Debate is polite disagreement.

All doors open to courtesy.

We teach our children our own manners.

Courtesy does not permit hatred, but contempt is fine.

Courtesy is that display of good manners your husband gets around other women.

The polite learn from the impolite.

If you must bow, bow low.

Courtesy is the contrivance of a wise man to keep fools at a distance.

Other times, other manners.

Courtesy is the mother of all the other virtues.

Be polite to everyone, you never know who might serve on the jury.

Table manners are for people who aren't hungry.

Be civil to all, sociable to many, and familiar with just a few.

It's polite to honk your horn before you force someone off the road.

Courtesy is the best defence.

In dogs, breeding. In men, manners.

Courtesy is offering your seat to a pregnant woman as you get off the bus.

What can you expect from a pig except a grunt?

Always be polite to your children, you may want to live with them one day.

Gratitude is the finest form of courtesy.

Courtesy is the ability to put up with bad manners without being rude.

Always thank polite people, and never assume it is merely their manner.

To be polite to superiors is mandatory, to equals decency, but to inferiors it shows nobility.

Diplomacy

Diplomacy misrepresents the greatest number of people.

Diplomacy is the art of skating over thin ice without getting into hot water.

A diplomat lays his cards on the table, but keeps the aces up his sleeve.

When a diplomat is being run out of town, he makes it look like he's leading the parade.

Diplomacy is the art of saying *nice doggie*, until you can find a rock.

Diplomacy is the art of letting someone else have your way.

Diplomats are people who go overseas to lie for the government.

Diplomacy is having the strength to leave the wrong thing unsaid at the most tempting moment.

When a diplomat says yes he means maybe, when he says maybe he means no, and when he says no, he's no diplomat.

Diplomacy is timing, you have to know when to shut your mouth before someone wants to shut it for you.

A diplomat acts disarming when his country is not.

It's the art of slicing up a cake and letting everyone think they're getting the big bit.

Diplomacy is the ability to say the nastiest things in the nicest possible way.

Diplomats are the essential element to starting wars.

To a diplomat, a disagreement is merely the basis of a future agreement.

A diplomat gets things off his chest while keeping his shirt on.

If you want to deceive a diplomat, tell him the truth. He'll never believe you.

He can juggle a hot potato long enough for it to become a cold issue.

Never mention a noose in a house where someone was hanged.

Diplomacy is the art of telling someone to go to hell in such a way that they look forward to the trip.

Tact is when you still make your guests feel at home, even though you wish they were.

Diplomacy is when opposing sides are eyeball to eyeball, and both simply blink.

Diplomacy is the art of removing the stinger from the bee without getting stung.

With roses, be a rose. With thorns, be a thorn.

It's the ability to insult someone in such a way they think it's a compliment.

Diplomacy is war by alternate methods.

Diplomacy is the ability to talk to every man as though you admired him, and every woman as though you desired her.

Diplomacy is the unsaid part of what you think.

It's the art of knowing how far is too far.

Diplomacy is having the willpower not to say what everyone is thinking.

It's the ability to convince ignorant people that they know more than you do.

Beneath what we say, lurks all that we know.

A diplomat is someone who can fight for what he wants with a smile on his face.

It's the art of handling a porcupine without disturbing its quills.

Diplomacy is the ability to inject someone without their being aware of it.

Diplomacy is most effective when people aren't allowed to talk about it.

Diplomacy is the art of lying in state.

It's when you think twice before saying nothing using a big vocabulary.

It's the ability to call someone a thief in such a way that he thanks you for bringing it to his attention.

Empathy

Empathy is the ability to understand how the horse feels when they give the cup to the jockey.

Empathy is having your pain in my chest.

We all somehow find the strength to bear the misfortune of others.

God, grant me the strength to cope with those who think they understand me.

Empathy is two hearts pulling the same load.

Your smile makes me happy, your pain hurts me.

Empathy is what you offer in exchange for all the juicy details.

If you truly want to understand something, try to change it.

The quality of the excuse you're offered for bad behaviour is an indication of what that person thinks of you.

Empathy is the opposite of compassion fatigue.

Miserable when you're miserable, happy when I'm away from you.

I can sympathise with everything, except suffering.

Empathy is the ability to appear sympathetic without appearing pathetic.

Empathy is cheaper than a loan.

What comes from the heart goes to the heart.

When you live near a cemetery, you soon learn not to cry every time you see a funeral procession.

I will groan for you, and you can moan for me.

Once a camel gets his nose in a tent, his body will follow.

Thirst cannot be quenched by proxy.

Never take a fence down before you know why it was put up.

If I can feel your sorrow, you can pity me too.

To understand is to forgive.

Empathy is the ability to see that old ruin in its former glory.

Personalise your sympathy, depersonalise your antipathy.

The tears we shed for others dry quickly.

Empathy gives you the edge in hurting others.

You're pathetic, and I'm sympathetic.

We love each other because we share the same symptoms.

Empathy is the ability to see the nail from the timber's point of view.

Don't sacrifice your heart on every altar.

Some are moulded by their admirations, others by their hostilities.

No-one limps because someone else's leg is hurt.

I know exactly how you feel.

Empathy works better without details.

One man's no is worth more than another man's yes.

Empathy is the sympathetic noises you make when you notice someone suffering.

Empathy is the sympathy you feign when you're too embarrassed to admit you couldn't care less.

Everyone was so concerned about the Titanic, no-one stopped to wonder how the iceberg felt.

Empathy is thinking with the heart.

I feel sorry for you, but I'm glad I'm not you.

Empathy is the ability to sympathise, without becoming emotionally involved.

Forgiveness

Turn the other cheek too far, and you'll get it in the neck.

Please forgive me now, in case I don't feel guilty later on.

Most of us can forgive and forget, we just don't want the other person forgetting that we forgave.

The trouble with forgiving and forgetting is the constant reminders.

Of course I'll forgive you, but that entitles me to reheat your sins for dinner at least once a week.

Who needs forgiveness more, the enemy who wronged you, or the friend who told you about it?

He who forgives too easily invites more offences.

Forget my past, but don't forget my present.

Of course I'll forgive you, but only until your next transgression.

It's easier to be forgiven than it is to seek permission.

I'm proud to say I've never forgiven anyone, even though I've never been quite as alone as I am now.

It's easy to forgive someone who is sufficiently miserable.

Forgiveness is as effective as putting a band-aid on a broken cup that's going to be immersed in hot water ever day.

We only stop forgiving when we stop loving.

A forgiving God is an unjust God.

Forgive those who have wronged you, but only after you get even.

Forgiveness assumes that something that was smashed to pieces can miraculously be mended with no memory of the repair.

Perhaps I can forgive, but I can never forget.

It may be noble to forgive, but it's not realistic.

It's much harder to forgive someone for being right.

He who does you wrong will never forgive you.

The biter will get bitten if he won't let go.

It's easier to forgive than it is to forget what you've forgiven.

Amnesty is when the hierarchy pardons others in return for their own injustices being overlooked.

Nothing makes sin as mighty as forgiveness.

If only it was possible to forgive, and then forget that you forgave.

Revenge makes you even, but forgiveness makes you superior.

Pardoning the bad is injuring the good.

The secret of forgiveness is misunderstanding.

There are formalities that should always be observed between even the closest of friends.

It is manlike to bear extremities, and godlike to forgive.

Forgive one offence and you encourage many others.

We cannot forgive others for not being like ourselves.

After a good meal, you can even forgive your relatives.

Don't rub it in, rub it out.

Of course God will forgive me, that's what he does for a living.

Transgression is written in sand, forgiveness is etched in marble.

Forgiveness takes the sting out of feeling guilty.

Humility

If I didn't make you look so bad, I wouldn't look so good.

It's good for a man to eat thistles and remember he is an ass.

No-one in the world is less egotistical than I am.

You don't need humility, you're just not that great.

None so empty as those who are full of themselves.

I cannot turn the other cheek because my tongue is already in it.

Life ultimately comes down to a choice between honest arrogance and hypocritical humility.

It's hard to be humble when you're as wonderful as I am.

God made man on the sixth day, after the flea.

Humility is the art of encouraging others to find out for themselves just how wonderful you are.

Humility is to genius what rain is to a candle.

My lack of humility is what keeps me from being absolutely perfect.

Humility is when you blush while you're boasting.

Humility is the realisation of the insignificance of human achievement.

Better a self confessed sinner than a self righteous saint.

I may not always be right, but I am never wrong.

Humility decreases with every promotion and completely evaporates at the top.

Everyone admires a humble man, if they ever hear of him.

The humbler I become, the more self righteous I grow.

The fuller it is, the lower it bends. The emptier it is, the taller it stands.

He who despises himself, esteems himself as a self-despiser.

A whale is harpooned only when it spouts.

Nothing is beneath you as long as it does not reduce your value in your own eyes.

The nobler a man is, the harder it is for him to suspect inferiority in others.

Self praise implies that you have reached your personal pinnacle.

Pride is what we have, pity is what others have.

Better a quiet death than a public humiliation.

Never underestimate a man who overestimates himself.

Too humble is half proud.

A proud man needs to conceal his vanity.

In heaven, an angel is nobody in particular.

Humility is a front for malice.

A weed is merely a plant whose virtues have not yet been discovered.

Meekness is the mask of malice.

Fans don't boo nobodies.

We are vain by nature and modest by necessity.

Yes-men can be bought.

Think small, be small.

Humility is that little space between too little and too much confidence.

He humbles himself to be exalted.

Hindsight is what a mistake looks like from behind.

The hen that lays the biggest egg cackles the least.

A humble person doesn't get carried away by the sound of his own mouth.

There is a point at which humility ceases to be a virtue.

Kindness

A kind soul has more footprints on it than a doormat.

If I was a cloud, I wouldn't rain on your parade.

Kind people attract freaks.

If you can't be kind, at least be vague.

Better a small posy now, than an extravagant wreath later.

Kindness consists of not asking what you can do, but of doing what you can.

The kind should be grateful to the cruel for providing a basis for comparison.

No-one is kinder than a king on his coronation day.

Good intentions die if they're not executed.

Be kind to nasty people, they need it more than most.

Kindness is a language even the deaf can hear.

Kind words can be spoken softly, but their echoes are endless.

Kindness can often accomplish what force cannot.

Kindness costs nothing but it's worth plenty.

One kind word can warm three winter months.

Kind words boomerang.

Even a milking cow appreciates warm hands.

It's human nature to keep tabs on what we've given.

Affirmative action is kindness to the point of condescension.

Kindness is the oil that takes the friction out of life.

I hate the giving of the hand unless the whole person accompanies it.

Kindness grows old fast.

Kindness makes the angels smile.

Kindness begins and often ends at home.

Nobody resents kind words.

Kindness sows the seeds of a smile.

It's easy to be kind to people you don't care about.

Kindness has a short life span.

No sentiment weighs as much as a kind action.

People are kinder that I thought they were, but less just.

I am kind because I hate being surrounded by miserable people.

We are made kind by being kind.

A kind word is better than a big pie.

A pat on the head achieves more than a kick in the rear.

Kind words inspire love.

Kindness is the ability to ignore ingratitude.

All cruelty springs from weakness.

Kindness is the capacity to be nice to those who don't deserve it.

I never forget a kindness, otherwise I'd never be repaid for it.

Cruelty is one of humanity's primitive pleasures.

Kind thoughts lead to kind deeds.

Be kind to him today, you may need him tomorrow.

You can't lift someone else up without rising yourself.

A man never looks better than when he stoops to help a child.

Be kind, God is omnipotent.

Sometimes we confuse kindness with what is useful.

Health

Diet

Not only was the food terrible, but the portions were tiny.

He said he hadn't had a bite in days, so I bit him.

I hate barbeques, I wouldn't have one in the house.

A refrigerator is where you keep your leftovers until you're ready to throw them out.

At the end of every diet, the path curves back to the trough.

Babe. If you enjoyed the movie, you're going to love eating the cast.

If you eat healthy, you'll die healthy.

Dieticians live off the fat of the land.

I didn't fight my way to the top of the food chain to be a vegetarian.

The noblest dog is the hot dog, which feeds the hand that bites it.

I think, therefore I overeat.

I asked for tea, but if this is tea, then I want coffee.

If God didn't want us to eat animals, why did he fill them with meat?

Food is an important part of any balanced diet.

So many cats, so few recipes.

Just when restaurant prices cease to be important, calories become the problem.

Hunger is not a debateable issue.

Tell me what you eat, and I'll tell you what you are.

Obesity snacks up on you.

I used to have a wonderful figure, but it's behind me now.

Garlic prolongs life, but you'll die lonely.

Too much of a good thing is wonderful.

Eating a chunk of stale bread is not dining.

She's so thin that when she closes one eye, she looks like a needle.

An hors-d'oeuvre is a ham sandwich cut into eight pieces and served on a bed of lettuce.

If you had to kill what you ate, you would probably be a vegetarian.

There is no such thing as a little garlic.

Hi, what's thawing?

When all else fails, eat.

We give the leftovers to the dog, and he gives them to the cat.

She was a good cook as good cooks go, but as good cooks go, she went.

There's more meat on a butcher's apron than there is in this stew.

The best way to serve tripe is to give it to someone else.

To a hungry man, any food will satisfy.

Tripe should be well cleaned, marinated, and thrown out.

If we are what we eat, that explains why there are so many fruits and nuts about.

To a starving man, a boiled turnip is as good as a roast chicken.

Why starve yourself to death just so you can live a little longer?

Eat peanuts, fifty million monkeys can't be wrong.

You never know what a poor loser you are until you go on a diet.

A good diet will take the starch out of you.

The Scarsdale Diet is when you shoot your doctor and spend the rest of your life on bread and water.

Doctors

They don't do much harm, considering the opportunities they have.

A doctor's mild discomfort is a patient's excruciating pain.

The purpose of a doctor is to prevent people from dying naturally.

A specialist is a doctor who thinks you have what he treats.

A doctor is a person who collects old magazines, which he keeps in a special room for sick strangers to read, while they wait for antibiotics.

When a patient is at death's door, it's up to the doctor to pull him through.

A quack is a medically unqualified person whose medicines kill people, whereas a doctor lets people die by themselves.

The ratio of killing to curing is rising rapidly.

There are worse occupations than feeling a woman's pulse.

What doesn't kill you makes you stronger, otherwise you die.

You should become a doctor, you make everyone sick.

I don't care if you've got a PhD, don't touch me.

Orthodontists spend hours looking a gift horse in the mouth.

Cured of disease, to die by a careless doctor.

Surgeons wear masks during operations so that they can't be identified when something goes wrong.

A general practitioner bases his diagnosis on the look of your tongue, and a psychiatrist bases his on the sound of your tongue.

Old doctors never die, they just lose their patients.

When all the doctors went on strike, the death rate dropped.

If I didn't pretend to cure, you'd die of despair.

Give orthopaedic surgeons a break.

Doctors revenge themselves for being the butt of so many jokes by charging a fortune.

Medicine may prolong life, but death will eventually get the doctor too.

If you really want a second opinion, come back tomorrow and I'll say it again.

A doctor distracts the patient while nature cures the illness.

Never consult a doctor whose office plants have died.

Dentists put metal in your mouth while extracting gold from your purse.

A doctor buries his mistakes.

A dentist always looks down at the mouth.

To be a good doctor, you must be absolutely sterile.

A specialist is a doctor with a small practice and a big income.

Nature heals, and the doctor gets paid.

An undertaker is someone who follows doctors.

Who shall decide when doctors disagree?

The doctor is really witty, he'll soon have you in stitches.

Only a doctor can get a woman to strip and bill her husband for it.

The best surgeon has many scars.

What your patient doesn't take, can't hurt him.

Natural immunity is the body's ability to catch a disease without the help of a doctor.

A patient is a body of pain surrounded by expensive specialists.

No doctor ever prescribes the most effective cure for illness, death.

Every doctor has his favourite cure.

Every invalid thinks he's a doctor.

Mental Health

Yesterday I was Napoleon. Today I'm nobody.

A psychiatrist is someone who asks expensive questions.

If someone doesn't find out what makes me tick soon, it's going to explode.

We're all out to get me.

Reality is a nightmarish illusion produced by drug deficiency.

I wouldn't be so paranoid if everyone would just stop picking on me.

Where am I now that I need me?

My faulty perception doesn't necessarily mean my conclusions are wrong.

Psychiatry is the science of pulling habits out of laboratory rats.

Freud put the anal into analysis.

Anyone who goes to a psychiatrist should have his head read.

Psychiatrists collect rent from patients who build castles in the air.

A psychiatrist is a talent scout for a mental institution.

Tell me your phobia, and I'll tell you what you're afraid of.

I'm not run down, I'm wound up.

I realised I was God when it suddenly occurred to me, as I was praying, that I was talking to myself.

Open my head and let them out.

Reality is a Rorschach ink blot.

There's nothing wrong with me, it's the world that's abnormal.

Don't let people drive you crazy, it's within walking distance.

What makes you tick, needs winding.

Reality is a withdrawal symptom.

I don't suffer from mental illness, I enjoy every single moment of it.

Support mental health, or I'll kill you.

It's not that I have an inferiority complex, it's just that everyone's better than me.

What sane person could live in this crazy world?

Beam me up, Scotty.

Just because I'm paranoid, doesn't mean they're not out to get me.

Every time I shut the door on reality, it sneaks back in through the air vents.

The shadows know.

Better to be mad and not know it, than to be sane and have your doubts.

The greatest oak was once a little nut who held its ground.

The plug's pulled out of the socket.

A sadist is someone who's terribly kind to a masochist.

The loose screw is the one that holds the tongue in place.

Mental health is enough to drive anyone crazy.

It's a mad mad world, and only the mad are sane.

He doesn't have an Oedipus complex, he just loves his mother.

Humpty Dumpty was pushed by the CIA.

I soar like an eagle, but I have trouble landing.

Mickey Mouse is really a rat who is out to get me, but nobody believes me.

The lift doesn't go all the way to the top floor.

Insanity is a perfectly rational adjustment to an insane world.

He's not what he's cracked up to be, he's nuts.

Only a madman knows the joy of insanity.

Physical Health

Good health is the slowest form of death.

Illness expands to meet the available budget.

Deep breathing kills germs, but it's difficult to get the germs to breathe deeply.

The older you get, the less space there is in the medicine cabinet.

You have to know what's wrong with you before you know which specialist to see.

A minor operation is one performed on someone else.

A prescription prolongs illness without endangering life.

These pills definitely aren't habit forming, I've been taking them for years.

A hypochondriac is a bed bug with imaginary pains.

Constipation is the thief of time, but diarrhoea waits for no man.

Threaten a man with amputation, and he'll be content to limp.

There is no instant cure, every wound heals by degrees.

The best thing for a man who has everything is penicillin.

Everyone studies disease, but no-one studies good health.

An ailing person lives forever.

The word *virus* is Latin for *I haven't got a clue.*

There's no such thing as a mild heart attack.

Sickness is when you don't feel good enough to act bad.

Evidence of medical progress is that your itch is now an allergy.

Bacteria is the culture doctors have.

Allergy is nothing to sneeze at.

I think I've temporarily given the pallbearers the slip.

Enemas put the wind up me.

One look at him and you have to wonder whether there were any other survivors.

Eschatology gives me the shits.

It's no longer about staying healthy, it's about your choice of disease.

Sickness gallops in and crawls out.

More people are dying of fatal diseases today than ever.

Medicare is a tax on health.

Some cures kill more than the disease.

Rhinitus gets up my nose.

Look after yourself and your body will last you a lifetime.

Hypochondria is the only disease I don't have.

A cough is something you can't help, but everyone else just does it to irritate you.

When you breathe in, you inspire. When you breathe out, you expire.

A virus is an illness with symptoms that defy modern medicine.

Medicare has brought expensive diseases within the reach of everyone.

To maintain a picture of health, use your frame of mind.

Show a sick man death, and he'll be content with fever.

We are aware of sickness, but never of health.

A long sleep and a good laugh are the best cures.

Speech therapists are all talk and no action.

Nothing makes you pay the dentist's outstanding bill faster than a new toothache.

What do you mean, don't start watching a soap opera?

If you feel like the morning after, but you haven't been anywhere, you're ill.

It's getting more and more difficult to find diseases I can afford.

Ideology

Activism

Britain's cowardly terrorists are Ireland's heroic freedom fighters.

A revolutionary is an oppressed person waiting for his turn to become the oppressor.

The activist knows only two positions, your foot on my neck, and my foot on your neck.

Today's activist is tomorrow's tyrant.

Death to all fanatics.

A rebel is a disillusioned conformist.

An activist only does what God would do if he had all the facts.

They begin by demanding justice and end by cracking the same whip.

It's not about the underprivileged, it's about the transfer of power from one elitist to another.

The sheep see the shepherd as their liberator, but the wolf is still hungry.

The worst enemies of the new radicals are the old liberals.

You can't stop a revolution with a referendum.

Explosives are appropriate where logic fails.

Lecturers inspire ideas that their students kill to implement.

If Jesus were here today, he would be a revolutionary.

Living it is much more dangerous than talking it.

A refugee is a person who votes with his feet.

All activists are orphans, whether they have a family or not.

Anarchy is the stepping stone to absolute power.

If you gained control through terrorism, you will retain control through terror.

Life is cheap. It's the accessories that are expensive.

Every successful activist sooner or later wears the same crown his predecessor wore.

Political power grows out of the barrel of a gun.

The acclaim he receives is earned by the blood of his followers.

It's hard to tell whether an activist is a smart man bluffing or an imbecile who means it.

Revolution is the end result of foreign aid.

The world sympathises with terrorists as long as they live far away.

No man can terrorise a nation unless the population become his accomplices.

If you're not satisfied with Moses, you have to accept Pharaoh's rule.

There is no room in an activist's mind for reason.

A fanatic keeps increasing his efforts long after he's forgotten his aim.

Revolutions are revolting.

Fanatics have the courage of their conviction, and the intolerance of their courage.

An activist loves humanity generally, but loathes people specifically.

You cannot enforce the laws against me, I make my own laws.

I always escape the fate of my adherents as I herd them to hell.

Those with power have the power to keep it.

Assassination is murder with a noble name, but it has replaced the vote in many countries.

There is always more hell than needed raising.

A tyrant is a slave turned inside out.

An activist is someone with a gun in his hand and both feet firmly planted in the air.

An activist progresses from preaching freedom to becoming a fanatical monomaniac.

Feminism

A feminist is a woman who wants breasts to replace the penis as a job qualification.

I have ceased to be a lady, but I am not yet a man.

Ginger Rogers did everything Fred Astaire did, only backwards and wearing high heels.

Give a woman a man's job and she grows balls.

Penis envy is a phallusy.

Equality is a myth, women are superior.

I am becoming the man I once wanted to marry.

I don't want a penis, just the privileges that go with it.

That useless piece of skin at the end of a penis is a man.

She's like a skunk, a pussycat with a secret weapon.

Some leaders just happen to be born women.

The most important jobs are still reserved for men, although the penis is not a recognised qualification.

She's a chip off the old glacier.

When a woman acts like a man, why is it never a gentleman?

A feminist is someone who doesn't live to serve.

The value of the penis isn't in its properties as a water toy, but in the social status it confers.

Women's Lib was designed to give women something to do in their spare time.

We are in the process of transforming breasts into a qualification for a better job.

The happiest people in the world are married men and single women.

He's not half the man his mother was.

Did you hear the rumour about the feminist who made a joke at her own expense?

Man was God's first attempt at creation, with woman he achieved perfection.

A pedestal is as much a prison as any small confined space.

A world without men would be full of fat, happy women.

I don't want equality, I want revenge.

We'll never be free before grammar is more important than glamour.

Macho doesn't prove mucho.

When a woman makes a fool out of a man, it's an improvement.

We think in generalities, but we live in detail.

If all men are born free, how come women are slaves?

Religion will be a feminist issue as long as we sing hymns and not hers, and say *amen* and not *awomen.*

When God created man, she overestimated her ability.

If God wanted us to think with our wombs, why did he give us brains?

Behind every successful man stands a woman who wants his job.

The head of the family should be firm, and she is.

Poor Eve, she's still being punished for Adam's weakness.

If men got pregnant, abortion would be a sacrament.

In some countries, women traditionally walked behind men, but this has changed in recent years, due mainly to the large quantity of unexploded land mines.

If Eve were here today, she would sue for defamation.

When God created man, she was only joking.

If some women don't have a sense of humour, it's so that they won't laugh at men.

Go braless, it pulls the wrinkles out of your face.

Idealism

I am a member of the meddle class.

Rent-a-crowd is a centipede, with a foot in every cause.

The idealist demands that his Thought Police monitor your ideas.

Ideology is the axle upon which world peace is precariously balanced.

When you're rowing, you haven't got time to rock the boat.

A martyr moves along the line of least resistance towards his desired death.

The end move is always to pick up a gun.

When in China, I preach capitalism. When in Australia, I preach communism.

Castles in the air are fine if you're not the one who has to live in them.

Ideology increases in proportion to the distance from the problem.

The less you have in common with the human race, the greater the notion of a brotherhood of man seems.

The line between hunger and anger is a thin one.

A desk is a dangerous place from which to view the world.

Every reform movement has a lunatic fringe.

We're so busy admiring dead martyrs that we neglect live heroes.

To kill for an ideal is to exaggerate the value of conjecture.

We must strive to silence those who oppose freedom of speech.

Liberty of any kind is never lost all at once.

I'm not a leftist, I'm where the righteous ought to be.

Intolerance of ambiguity is the mark of an authoritarian.

The value of an ideal has nothing to do with the sincerity of the one expressing it.

Idealists are always willing to make others into martyrs.

I love mankind, it's people I hate.

Idealists always claim to know what God wants them to do for the nation.

The worst cause can succeed with a good pleader.

The loudest proponents never offer their fortunes in support of other's causes.

The note struck by ideology vibrates in eternity.

The belief that your mission is divine is an affliction.

At twelve I was a socialist, at twenty I was a communist, but at forty I became a capitalist.

A riot is a mass demonstration of authority's ineffectual oppression.

Words, words, words.

A rose smells sweeter than an onion, so it's obviously more nutritious.

There are always other countries willing to pay for the guns we need.

A mob is a crowd whipped up into a collective frenzy.

Ideology is adaptable.

A liberal is a rich person whose material interests aren't at stake.

I may disagree with what you have to say, but I shall defend to the death, your right to say it.

Idealists ladle the ocean into their own private pond.

He's so busy cleaning up his neighbours' yards that he neglects his own.

A bigot is someone who doesn't agree with me.

From a safe distance, the armchair humanitarian loudly proclaims policy.

It works better in speeches than in reality.

A radical is a man with both feet firmly planted in the air.

Patriotism

I'm willing to die for my country, even if it kills me.

If you want a symbolic gesture don't burn the flag, wash it.

Patriotism stops at the border, where prejudice begins.

The promised land always looks better from a distance.

If he refers to our country as the arsehole of the world, don't worry. He's obviously just passing through.

Beautiful or not, this is my country. Related or not, he is my countryman.

Dual nationality is hyphenated citizenship.

Australia wouldn't be in such a mess if the Aboriginals had adopted tougher immigration laws in the first place.

Of course it's the best country in the world, I was born here.

Sometimes treason is true patriotism.

Patriotism is an individual's willingness to kill or be killed for trivial reasons.

I am truly cosmopolitan. I would be unhappy anywhere.

Be patriotic, question authority.

To a multiculturalist, Australia is merely another insignificant suburb of the world.

My country is the world, my countrymen are mankind, but I love no-one specifically.

Patriotism isn't a frenzied outburst against others, it's the steady personal dedication of a lifetime.

Patriotism is loving your choice, even when you had nothing to choose from.

Out of mutual failure or success, is born the national character.

If you really want to improve Australia, emigrate.

Patriotism is loyalty to your country, regardless of who is in power.

To sing the national anthem is an act of patriotism.

Multiculturalism has made patriotism a confusing issue.

Patriotism is partisan solidarity.

What this country needs is fewer people telling us what this country needs.

The accent lives on in the mind and on the lips.

A nationalist has a broad hatred and a narrow love.

A citizen of the world is faithful to no country.

My fatherland can beat your motherland any time.

A city has a face, a country has a soul.

Multiculturalism is when you reap the benefits of your new country, while maintaining loyalty to your old country.

I defend myself by defending my country.

New Zealand should never be incorporated into Australia. Two union jacks on the same flag would look ridiculous.

A patriot is someone who can take the politics out of patriotism.

Patriotism is the egg from which war is hatched.

True patriotism belongs to no political party.

There's no such thing as a hungry patriot.

Patriotism is pride of tribalism.

Even if Indonesia invades us, they can't all afford to live here.

The colours of the flag don't run.

In war, the loudest patriots profit the most.

I love Australia too much to be a nationalist.

Integrity

Conscience

Conscience is the moral man's evil-filter.

Conscience is what makes you hesitate before doing something bad.

Guilt is the punishment conscience extracts.

Conscience doesn't usually kick up much of a fuss until after you've done it.

The bigger the offence, the worse the torment.

There is another within me that is angry with me.

Conscience is the bill God sends you for bad behaviour.

Surely I deserve recognition for the bad things I haven't done.

It makes me feel bad to know I didn't feel worse.

Conscience is the inner being that hurts after the rest of you had a particularly good time.

Silence isn't always golden, sometimes it's guilt.

Developers do have a conscience. When they destroy trees to build a housing estate, they name the streets after what they've destroyed, like Elm and Oak.

Conscience is what makes you own up before someone tells on you.

I have reached that bridge I was going to cross when I got to it.

A good conscience sleeps through thunder.

We recognise bad behaviour by the flashes of remorse it inflicts on us.

Conscience is like a mother-in-law whose visit is eternal.

I would rather be strongly wrong than weakly right.

Conscience is that inner pest that taunts you when you know you've done wrong.

Conscience has many witnesses.

Humanity is guilty of allowing guilty men to pretend they're innocent.

His conscience fits into a flea's navel, and there's still room for his heart.

Conscience is when your mind feeds off itself.

Conscience is the pulse of reason.

Conscience can nag worse than a bitter spouse.

If you're at war with yourself, how can you find peace with others.

Conscience scolds like a disappointed parent.

How you sleep has more to do with conscience than a bad pillow.

Those who feel guilty feel afraid, and those who are afraid, feel guilty.

A guilty man runs even when no-one is chasing him.

It's just another word for decency.

The worm of conscience never needs to sleep.

A good conscience pays badly.

Conscience is when you ignore your good actions and concentrate on your bad ones.

Amendment is repentance.

Conscience is when you prey on yourself.

The unhappiest people are those who cannot forgive themselves.

The most painful wound is that little stab of conscience.

That creepy feeling you get when you're alone is your conscience catching up with you.

Nothing promotes a clear conscience like a bad memory.

Conscience is the hat misery doesn't want guilt to wear.

Never ask to be forgiven before you're accused, it pronounces you guilty.

Trust

In God we trust, but everyone else pays cash.

One moment of indiscretion can destroy a lifetime of trust.

Trust in Allah, but tie your camel.

Don't lie to me unless you're sure I'll never find out.

A promise made is a debt unpaid.

Of course you can trust me, but then, I'm only responsible for my own actions.

Accepting everything as God's will is just another way of saying you're happy to take a chance.

Better to deny at once, than to promise forever without delivering.

Those who have been betrayed, treat trust seriously.

Too trusting loses before the race begins.

It is difficult to trust someone who has no faith in his own ability.

Never place your trust in the future, it doesn't deserve it.

If you want to trust someone, you usually have to overlook minor discrepancies.

Never trust the teller, trust the tale.

I don't feel guilty about breaking promises, just surprised that people are that gullible.

Public trust is public property.

The same hand that feeds the piglet, hold the knife that slaughters it when grows older.

Would you buy a used car from this man?

I trust you completely, but please send cash.

Trust is the name of an honest man's reputation.

Much jealousy, little trust.

If you only trust yourself, no-one can betray you.

The best friend who once betrayed you becomes your worst enemy.

Poor trust is dead, bad pay killed him.

Never trust a repentant drunk.

There are few of us who are above the influence of gain.

Distrust is the only defence against betrayal.

When you know little, you suspect much.

It is a fault to trust everyone, and an equal fault to trust no-one.

I trust you no further than I can throw you.

Trust is revered, and yet it's allowed to die of hunger.

Never put it in writing.

Complete trust is a child's emotion.

Trust is dead, betrayal killed him.

Trust yourself only.

Trust everyone, but always shuffle the cards yourself.

Never trust anyone who tells you all their troubles, but shares none of their blessings.

Between friends, always have two witnesses and a notary.

If he cannot be trusted, he has no value.

Never trust anyone who tells half-truths, you never know which half he's told you.

Trust only those who have as much to lose as you do.

God protect me from those I trust.

There is honour amongst thieves.

When you do business with family, be polite but always have a witness present.

Not to trust another is to protect yourself against betrayal.

Intellect

Education

I've taught you everything I know, and you're still ignorant.

Education tampers with natural ignorance.

Teaching transfers notes from teacher to student, without passing through the minds of either.

God made idiots for practice before he made teachers.

School is bad enough, but at least I'm not letting them teach me anything.

The more I read Socrates, the less I wonder why they poisoned him.

Universities train us, but we educate ourselves.

Knowledge is not what you can remember, it's what you can't forget.

Support teachers, they work hard to raise the standards of illiteracy.

There are three kinds of mathematicians, those who can count, and those who can't.

Those who can't teach, teach the teachers.

It takes five years to recover from a university education.

As long as there are tests, children will pray.

Teachers teach other people's ideas, but we have to think for ourselves.

You can buy an education, but wisdom is a gift.

Education is when you're given answers to remember, rather than problems to solve.

Professors do it by degrees.

Teachers earn a lot and think a little.

Education has it's foundation in perception.

They're so busy teaching children to count, that they neglect to teach them what counts.

Learning is not compulsory, neither is survival.

It's better to ask twice than to get it wrong once.

It's not what you know, it's how you use that knowledge.

If a little knowledge is dangerous, we live in a perilous world.

Numeracy doesn't count these days.

As our knowledge increases, we realise how little we know.

We are all born princes, and then education turns us into frogs.

Education is its own reward.

Get a good education and you get rich quick, but only if you marry an heiress.

The obligation to endure gives us the right to know.

He who doesn't know one thing, knows another.

Never let anyone else do your homework for you. Get it wrong yourself.

It's what you learn after you know it all that counts.

True knowledge is knowing that you know nothing, but that in itself is knowledge.

Education is the journey from cocksure ignorance to thoughtful uncertainty.

We leave school with a bellyful of words, knowing nothing.

Education doesn't alter your problems, it just lifts them to a higher plane.

The purpose of education is to replace an empty head with an open mind.

Never let your schooling get in the way of your education.

Education is a progressive discovery of your own ignorance.

An academic devises solutions that will never be implemented, to problems that will never exist.

Humour

Some things are so serious that you can only joke about them.

I used to know a funny version of that joke.

You might as well laugh at yourself once in a while, everyone else does.

I'm deadly serious, it was a light-hearted joke.

Call yourself a comedian? Don't make me laugh.

Today's tragedy is tomorrow's joke.

One man's joke is another man's insult.

A sense of humour is what breaks tension before tension breaks you.

Truly funny people always have a tragic past.

If you can laugh at it, you can live with it.

It's easy to make people laugh, especially when you have most of the government working with you.

If you can't laugh at yourself, make fun of other people.

Humour is the first thing to vanish in a foreign tongue.

Blessed is the man who can laugh at himself, for he shall live in an amusement park forever.

It's a rare man who can laugh at himself with others, and enjoy the laugh as much as they do.

Laughter is the music of the soul.

Humour reduces horror to manageable proportions.

The secret source of humour is sorrow.

The hippopotamus is living proof that God has a sense of humour.

Fear often becomes humorous in hindsight.

Sarcasm is the sour cream of wit.

It's always funny when it happens to someone else.

Good taste and humour are a contradiction in terms, like a chaste whore.

Differences in humour strain relationships.

Brevity is the soul of wit.

Laughter is a tranquiliser without side effects.

A little nonsense now and then is cherished by the wisest men.

Satire is a joke.

Humour is the ability to ridicule your own imperfections.

Laughter feels good all over, but it shows in the face.

Comedy is a tragedy with a time lapse.

Sharp witted humour has a sting.

When a harnessed horse neighs, he's laughing at the thought of humans adjusting their seat belts.

Learn to laugh at trouble or you'll have a miserable old age.

Humour wounds some and heals others.

A day without laughter is wasted.

I'd rather laugh at something insane, than go insane because I can't laugh at it.

Laugh at everything, or be obliged to cry over everything.

He who laughs last, thinks slowest.

No-one is more profoundly sad than he who laughs the most.

You can't stay angry with someone who makes you laugh.

Laughter is a force of nature.

Ignorance

Of course everyone has the right to act stupid, but you abuse the privilege.

Lord, forgive me my nonsense the way I forgive the nonsense of those who think they're talking sense.

If you said hello, he'd be stuck for an answer.

Never have so many understood so little about so much.

There is no dunce like a mature dunce.

The lab called, your brain is ready.

If ignorance is bliss, you must be the happiest person in the world.

I'm not illiterate, my parents were definitely married.

Those who know nothing, know it the loudest.

You're obviously not the sharpest tool in the shed.

What's on your mind, if you'll pardon the exaggeration?

If he had twice as much sense, he would be an idiot.

It's better to remain silent and be thought a fool, than to speak and remove all doubt.

Imbeciles are the happiest people.

Better to cry with a wise man than to laugh with a fool.

An ignorant person is someone who doesn't know what I just found out.

A rich fool and his money are soon married.

I have to ask, are you really that stupid, or are you having me on?

An educated fool is worse than an ignorant one.

I would rather have my own ignorance than someone else's intelligence, because I've got so much to offer.

Some people are gifted with stupidity.

Ignorance is the mother of research.

A fool at forty is a fool indeed.

He took too many knocks on the head without his helmet on.

He can't meet an amputee without talking about shoes.

Nothing is fool proof, because fools are ingenious.

His train of thought is a string of empty carriages.

If you don't know anything, keep it to yourself.

Everyone makes a fool of themselves sometimes, but some exceed their quota.

He doesn't know that he doesn't know what he means.

There is always one more idiot than you counted on.

If the blind lead the blind, both will fall into a ditch.

Stupidity is a boundless concept.

To be aware of your own stupidity is the first step towards knowledge.

No-one is so stupid that others can learn nothing from him.

Never argue with a fool. If anyone's watching, they may not be able to tell which is which.

You have a one-track mind and there's no traffic.

He had a good idea once, but it died in solitary confinement.

The reason he always has that stupid smile on his face is that he's stupid.

The little I know, I owe to my ignorance.

Accumulated knowledge is a mind overloaded by its own ignorance.

Perpetual ignorance equals perpetual bliss.

Ignorance is a blank sheet upon which nothing has been written.

Imagination

Reality is terrific, but you wouldn't want to live there.

Once a mind has been stretched by new ideas, it never regains its original dimensions.

You find what you think you see, even if it's not there.

When I was younger I could remember anything, whether it happened or not.

It's the ability to think like yourself so that you can remember where you put something.

You can't rely on your judgement if your imagination is out of control.

If you jump off the edge, you just might find you can fly.

Fantasy is not an escape from reality, it's a way of understanding it.

Curiosity is creativity on its way to discovery.

The more we imagine, the more we must think we see.

Choosing is difficult for those with imagination.

Both of my childhood friends were imaginary, and neither of them would play with me.

Imagination is when a poet and a liar are put in charge of a warehouse of facts.

Reality is a collective hunch.

Dream as if you'll live forever. Plan as if you'll die today.

Inspiration is the memory of an event not yet experienced.

An idea isn't responsible for the people who believe in it.

Sit down and switch the ignition on.

It's not important what you believe, only that you do believe.

Imagination sometimes survives bad training.

The romance of the soul with nature is what creates imagination.

Doubt is the panic of a timid imagination.

A hunch is creativity trying to tell you something.

A solitary fantasy can transform a million realities.

Imagination can beat reality any time.

All that we are is the result of all that we have thought.

Mystery and imagination are the source of all great discoveries.

I know many things that aren't so.

The person who listens patiently to reason, is thinking of a way to refute it.

It's not what you look at that matters, it's what you see.

No genius ever had ignition problems.

Anyone can come up with a brilliant idea, but it takes a genius to make it work.

Imagination is the chief feature of a functioning brain.

Imagination is our defence in the war against reality.

Some of my clearest memories never actually happened.

Imagination gallops on ahead, while reality plods on slowly behind.

Knowledge is limited, but imagination encircles the world.

Imagination is the ability to dream while you're awake.

A library is an arsenal of liberty.

The space within is the reality of the space without.

All the things we've forgotten re-emerge as dreams.

Everything you can imagine, can be real.

Imagination is worth far more than education.

Imagination allows us to interpret what we see.

Imagination allows you to look through either side of the telescope.

Many a good idea has been buried under words.

You shouldn't let your mind wander off, it's too little be on its own.

Intelligence

A prodigy is a talented child with pushy parents.

I have an idea. You must be so proud.

You almost make me wish I had a lower IQ so that I could enjoy your company.

A fool with a university degree is an educated idiot.

In just a few weeks, a laboratory rat can train a scientist to bring it food every time it presses the buzzer.

Education isn't proof of intelligence, it's proof of the ability to mimic others.

A parrot repeats what it hears, but it lacks the ability to analyse what it's learned.

Ordinary men lament the lack of difference between people, intelligent people celebrate the differences.

At eighteen we know everything. Fifty years later even the questions confuse us.

The difference between genius and stupidity is that genius has limits.

Don't develop your own ideas, use mine.

An intellectual uses bigger words to tell you more than he knows.

So what if your child graduated with honours? You're still an idiot.

He's very clever, but his brains have gone to his head.

You can't teach people anything they don't want to know.

We distrust the heart too much, and the head not enough.

If it wasn't for the wheel, we'd still be dragging the cart.

The life of an illiterate man is death.

Genius is mental power, talent is how it's applied.

Education is homogenised intelligence.

Never engage in a battle of wits against someone who isn't an intellectual equal, because it's cruel to attack the unarmed.

The man who thinks he knows it all has simply stopped thinking.

Education is intelligence with the ability to think for yourself removed.

Intelligence is useless if it isn't put into practical use.

They educate us in their own image.

The greatest minds suffer most from their own limitations.

Genius is one percent inspiration and ninety nine percent perspiration.

If confusion is the first step towards knowledge, I'm on the road to genius.

The mind resorts to reason for lack of training.

An intellectual is an impractical person.

In the republic of mediocrity, genius is dangerous.

Common sense is the collection of prejudices acquired by the age of eighteen.

The stupid think it's all been done, the intelligent can't wait to start doing it.

Genius comes in a cracked container.

The chief cause of my anguish is another man's brilliance.

At a certain age your mind closes and you live on intellectual fat.

Genius is sacrificed to talent every day.

An intellectual is someone who is able to read books.

Intelligence will give you a better living than education will.

If it wasn't for Thomas Edison, we would be watching television by candlelight.

When brains are needed, muscles won't do.

Genius does what it must, talent what it can.

Memory

Have I found a rope, or lost a horse?

Memory Lane is wonderful because we can detour around the rough spots.

I'll never forget old what's-his-name.

Never remember what you can afford to forget.

Memory enhances trifles and reduces tragedies.

How can I remember your birthday when you never look any older?

Memory is the thing we forget with.

Memory is a card index system where the reference is never correctly replaced after being consulted.

As I said before, I never repeat myself.

She has a terrible memory. She never forgets a damn thing.

In memory it all happens to beautiful music, and it doesn't hurt.

You have a mind like a steel trap, what goes in never comes out again.

Amnesia is best forgotten.

To forget is routine.

Education is supposed to be about developing the mind, not cramming the memory.

I do have a photographic memory, although I occasionally forget about the lens cover.

I have forgotten more than you remember.

Do I remember? Can I ever forget?

Memory is the implement God uses to punish us with.

I live in the hope of becoming a memory.

Don't burden sweet memories of love with sour resentments.

Memory is when everyone you meet looks like someone else.

I don't want to remember, but I can't forget.

Amnesia is nature's way of saying *forget it.*

It's better to smile and forget than to remember and cry.

Memory is a diary we carry around with us.

A strong memory is linked to infirm judgement.

We don't remember days, we remember moments.

On good days, bad days are far away.

Women and elephants never forget.

What we've forgotten cries out to be remembered in dreams.

The joys and sorrows of life lie in memories.

To remember the past is to suffer twice.

An elephant never forgets, but then, how much does he have to remember?

Memory is when you later recall more than actually happened at the time.

When you lend money to a friend, you damage his memory.

Memory grows or shrinks at its owner's convenience.

What was unbearable is easier to remember.

Memory is what tells you that you know someone, but doesn't tell you who they are.

When I am tired, the memories I thought I had conquered long ago, attack me.

If only I had control over my memory.

Better to forget in happiness that to remember in sorrow.

Memory is what makes you wonder what you've forgotten.

You never know how much a politician can't recall until he's asked to testify.

The worst memory is of the time you were happy.

Justice

The Courts

Bail is when the jury gets locked up, and the criminal goes home to his family.

Murder is an act of God under suspicious circumstances.

Manslaughter is when the accused murders someone by accident.

If you offer a criminal $100 or thirty days, of course he's going to take the money.

So much evidence is suppressed that the jury have to guess which way the criminal went by looking at the intersection.

A jury referees the competition between two parties to decide who has the best lawyer.

You can tell the courts are getting tough because criminals are getting much longer suspended sentences.

A plea bargain is when you end a sentence with a proposition.

A jury is a group of twelve people who will try anyone once.

When you listen to evidence in court, it makes you wonder about history.

The judge is a midget, just another small thing sent to try me.

Every time the accused tries to tell the truth in court, his lawyer objects.

Even when it's used correctly, legalese is incomprehensible.

There are ways to settle the matter out of court, but you'd only be re-arrested.

A judge is a law student who marks his own examination papers.

A fixed jury never works right.

A trial doesn't prove guilt or innocence, just whether the prosecution or the defence had the better argument.

Judges are men of conviction.

Poor little perpetrator, nasty victim.

A man is presumed guilty until proven guilty, and then they let him go.

Punishment has less to do with the crime than the defence a criminal offers.

The price of freedom is wealth and good publicity.

A trial is not a quest for the truth, but the resolution of a dispute.

This is a court of law, what did you expect, justice?

A jury consists of twelve people who couldn't convince the judge they couldn't serve because of personal commitments.

The courts are doing a marvellous job. The prisons are full.

One murderer is more lenient towards another murderer.

Set a thief to catch a thief, and the jury will let him go.

The wages of sin vary considerably. Murderers walk free, and thieves go to jail.

The judicial system is no excuse for ignorance of the law.

A litigant is a person who forfeits his privacy to save his freedom.

A man is presumed guilty until he's proven influential.

We judge men by their worst moments in life, but some men's lives are one long continuous worst moment.

A precedent is when you show how two entirely different situations are identical.

Suppression is nine points of the law.

Times have changed. We now leave justice to God, and mercy to the courts.

The injury we suffer, and the injury we do, are not measured on the same set of scales.

The jury's task is to judge the car by the sound of its horn.

Justice

Amnesty is an act of compassion, which the government exercises only when the prisons are full.

They keep making new laws, although we already have more than we can break.

Someone only has to say, *there ought to be a law against it,* and there is.

Justice increases in accordance with the amount invested in it.

The law is a net strong enough to catch sardines, but too weak to hold a whale.

Justice is a decision in your favour.

To condemn someone for tax evasion is to condemn them for something they didn't do.

If your job is to clean out a sewer, you soon lose your sense of smell.

The death penalty doesn't eliminate crime, but it does stop repeat offenders.

Who will protect us from our protectors?

And what does the crime have to do with the criminal?

Law exists for the protection of the powerful, and the punishment of the small.

The more laws they pass, the more they erode our freedom.

So much law, so little justice.

All necessary evils began as justifiable measures and ended as infallible precedents.

New laws are followed by new tricks.

What is law is not justice, and what is justice is against the law.

We get the justice we can afford.

The law is blind and speaks in general terms.

Law maintains injustice.

So many laws, so much lawlessness.

The law is made by the conquerer, and imposed on the conquered.

New lords, new laws.

Justice is the sanction of established injustice.

The law is no good even when it is used lawfully.

There is justice for all, but it's not evenly distributed.

Many superfluous laws dilute the power of the few essential laws.

Justice is a question of technicalities.

There should be more laws to protect me from myself.

Good men need no laws, and bad men are indifferent to them.

Today even the most mediocre lawyer could find loopholes in the ten commandments.

People say justice when they mean wealth.

The fools make the laws that other fools obey.

Justice is not only deaf, dumb and blind, but it has a wooden leg.

The law will protect anyone who can afford it.

Practice doesn't make perfect, but it makes rich.

Condemn the system that acquits the guilty.

The law is a patient ass if you use a golden bridle.

Everyone demands justice in the affairs of another.

One law for the rich, another for the poor.

The law serves the law.

Amnesty is when you set old prisoners free, to make room for new ones.

Any fool can make a law, and usually does.

Do not decree what you cannot enforce.

Honesty is the best policy, but insanity is a better plea.

Lawyers

A lawyer is the larval stage of a politician.

The ideal weight of a lawyer is about five hundred grams, including the urn.

Bail in, bale out.

So many lawyers, so few bullets.

You can hire a lawyer's outrage.

I don't like to speak ill of the dead, but he was a real lawyer of a man.

I once knew someone who knew someone who once knew an honest lawyer.

Hell hath no fury like the lawyer of a woman scorned.

Changing lawyers is like moving to a different deck chair on the Titanic.

My job is to transform the perpetrators into the victims.

Every man is innocent in his lawyer's eyes.

Divorce is a game played by lawyers.

No lawyer will ever get to heaven while there's room in hell.

Lawyers interpret the law, and no two speak the same language.

A legacy is a dead give away.

A lawyer still takes you to the cleaners even if you've lost your suit.

If I had but one life to give for my country, it would be my lawyer's life.

He's willing to spend your last dollar to prove he's right.

A lawyer's mouth doesn't open until you put money in it.

A bad agreement is still better than a good lawyer.

Lawyers who specialise in divorce live happily ever after.

Old lawyers never die, they just lose their appeal.

The best thing in life is fee.

For God so wanted to punish humanity that he created lawyers.

A lawyer is someone who helps you get what's coming to him.

The difference between a lawyer and a catfish is that one is a scum sucking bottom dweller and the other one is a fish.

A lawyer's opinion is worth nothing unless it's paid for.

There are only three jokes about lawyers, the other stories are all true.

You have a good strong case. How much justice can you afford?

Alive or dead, sooner or later you're going to need me.

Criminals are stupid because there are so many legal ways to steal.

Virtue in the middle, said the devil, as he sat down between two lawyers.

Although he became a lawyer, his parents were married when he was born.

Always hire a rich lawyer.

No writer ever took as many liberties with the truth as lawyers do.

A lawyer who defends himself has a fool for a client.

A good lawyer is a terrible neighbour.

Utter waste is when a busload of lawyers goes over a cliff with three empty seats.

To break a contract is to undertake to overthrow an undertaking.

A lawyer's house is built on the gullibility of fools.

Black always look good on a lawyer, like a Doberman, for instance.

The cemetery is full of good lawyers.

What I loathe today, I love tomorrow, according to my client's needs.

A lawyer enables his client to do what he likes, but isn't legally entitled to do.

Lawyers don't go to hell because they don't have souls.

Leisure

Entertainment

A small role is better than a long loaf.

One of my biggest regrets was that I could never sit in the audience and watch myself.

I climbed to the heights of success, and teetered on the pinnacle of fame.

I don't deserve this applause, but what's my opinion compared with those who know better?

The entertainment scene is the same old same old, last picture, next husband.

So much confidence, so little talent.

You can identify an entertainer by the glazed look they get when the conversation wanders away from their latest production.

A critic is someone who stones the first cast.

Why only twelve disciples? With our budget, we could have hundreds.

The reaction of the audience is fifty percent of the performance.

If you can fake sincerity, you've got it made.

When I need to make myself cry, I think about my love life.

An actor is a show oaf.

All comedies end with marriage, and marriage ends all comedies.

What we want in entertainment is an escape from reality, not more blood and guts.

An agent believes his clients steal ninety percent of his income.

Acting is the lowest form of art.

I was married to an entertainer until I caught him in the act.

I don't mind if someone looks at his watch during my performance, but it annoys me when he keeps putting it to his ear to see if it's stopped.

On stage he is a natural, off stage he acts terribly.

The audience was with me all the way, until I finally managed to shake them off.

Just remember your lines and don't knock anything over.

I knew her before she was a virgin.

Every production resembles its author.

A comedian knows a good joke when he steals one.

He's destined to go far, and the sooner the better.

The purpose of live theatre is to silence the audience.

Fred Astaire was old and wrinkled and smelled of ginger.

My agent has dozens of offices overseas, so I'm unemployed in at least eleven countries.

Theatre is the art of keeping a large group of people from coughing.

Strip away the tinsel, and there's real tinsel underneath.

Applause is a duty, laughter is a reward.

Movies are entertainment made for the half-witted masses by the morally corrupt few.

Censorship assumes that what you don't know can hurt you.

Egged on by ambition, egged off by audience.

The best ideas come from jokes. Think funny.

When subtlety fails, use cream pies.

She couldn't carry a tune if it had handles.

He only had two expressions, hat on and hat off.

Hollywood has more stars than heaven.

Leisure

I'm not fishing, I'm teaching my worm to swim.

Despite what critics say, if television allows mothers a few hours' relaxation at the pub, how can it be all bad?

Fishing is an uninhabited body of water surrounded by liars in old clothes.

Colour television? I wouldn't believe it until I saw it in black and white.

Leisure is the ability to hear a tap leak and do nothing about it.

Television has changed children from an irresistible force into an immovable object.

Excess is fine, as long as you do it in moderation.

Dancing is a perpendicular expression of horizontal desire.

A hobby is hard work that you wouldn't want to do for a living.

When you throw your dog a ball to fetch, he's entertaining you too.

I fully intend to do something with my leisure time, as soon as I get around to it.

The time you enjoyed wasting wasn't wasted at all.

When a habit begins to cost a lot of money, we call it a hobby.

If you slave away in the hot sun while I surf, we both still get around the world at the same rate.

We spend too much time reading the menu instead of enjoying the banquet.

If God didn't want men to fish, he wouldn't have invented fishing rods.

Give me a set of golf clubs, fresh air, and a beautiful woman, and you can keep the golf clubs.

Television is the thief of time.

Sunday drivers don't necessarily drive any better during the week.

The test of pleasure is the memory it leaves behind.

The time you wasted not fishing you just frittered away on nothing.

If it wasn't for television, the divorce rate would be much higher.

I go to the opera regularly, whether I need a nap or not.

We spend half our lives trying to figure out what to do with the time we've saved.

Never put off till tomorrow what you can put off for good.

Bubble bath, there's no place like foam.

I hate television as much as I hate peanuts, but I can't give them up either.

Soap opera, corn on the sob.

Television is radio with eyestrain.

Television has changed conversation into a debate about what to watch.

The boss says when and the family says where, and yet they call it a holiday.

A holiday is having nothing to do, and all day to do it in.

Fishing is a smelly way of taking it easy.

Fishing is a jerk at one end of the line, waiting for a jerk at the other end.

Solitude is much more enjoyable when you have someone to share it with.

Television induces a coma without the expense, worry or inconvenience.

Nothing makes a fish grow faster than almost being caught.

Never put off till tomorrow what you can do the day after tomorrow.

As relaxed as empty gloves.

Idle people have the least leisure.

Television enables millions of lonely people to watch the same programme at the same time, without the prospect of alleviating anyone's loneliness.

There are toys for all ages.

Retirement

Retirement is twice as much husband on half as much money.

They say retirement adds ten years to your life, and I'd like to spend those extra years working.

I can no longer afford to waste my time making money.

What happens to the hole when the cheese is finished?

The pension is mightier than the job.

Work is an invasion of privacy.

At my age, I can afford to be unemployed.

A retired husband is his wife's full time job.

I've suddenly discovered that work is more fun than fun.

But I can rest all I like once I'm dead.

I'm now at that stage where I have to prove that I'm just as good as I never was.

A man retires, but a woman just keeps right on cooking and cleaning.

Retirement is leisure with dignity.

I retired for a retread, so I can go off in a different direction.

Finally, I'm in the business of living for myself.

A retired person has finally learned enough to be considered useless.

I don't know what we're going to do without you, but we're going to try.

Well, I can't stand around here talking to you for hours, people will think I'm on a coffee break.

Retirement eliminates your reasons for getting out of bed in the morning.

Retirement is when you've finally learned that you'll never have enough money for all

The biggest burden is having nothing to carry.

You've always been shy, but now you're retiring.

Retirement causes a caustic tongue.

What do I do for a living? As little as possible.

At sixty-five a man is sufficiently experienced to lose his job.

Hard work never hurt anyone who hired someone else to do it.

Retirement is when your wife takes over all those jobs your secretary used to do. Well, almost all.

Nobody ever drowned in his own sweat.

My job was me, and now I no longer know who I am.

Retirement negates your previous profession.

Retire while you still have some snap in your garters.

You mean this is what I worked all my life to achieve?

Absence of occupation is not rest.

He's irreplaceable, mainly because no-one seems to know what he did.

Retirement is when you don't do all the things you said you were going to do when you had the time.

I was going to play golf seven times a week, instead I wash dishes three times a day.

When you retire and time is no longer relevant, the company gives you a gold watch.

Retirement is not so much losing a worker, as gaining a parking space.

Dismiss the old mule in good time, before anyone laughs at his feeble efforts.

You can only hold your stomach in for so many years.

We work all our lives to be able to retire comfortably, only to find retirement unbearable.

Sports

Paraplegics, stand up for your rights.

It isn't about playing the game, it's about keeping the score.

Thanks to jogging, more people are dying at the peak of fitness.

Athletes run in the family.

If God had meant us to touch our toes, he would have put them near the belly button.

Skydiving, good to the very last drop.

I run scared, raise my hopes and push my luck.

You can't win the big one if you don't win the little ones first.

It's not about winning or losing, it's about how you look while you play.

You get a piece of paper for years of hard study, and a gold medal for running fast once.

Love means nothing to a tennis player.

Defeat is worse than death, because you have to live with the adverse publicity afterwards.

Boxers are ninety percent scar tissue.

If you can't do it well, enjoy doing it badly.

I keep fit by exercising, up down, left right, and now the other finger.

By the time you learn to play well, the selectors think you're too old to make the team.

If he didn't raise his eyebrows, he would never get any exercise.

Of course I exercise, last week I was out four nights running.

It's only a game until someone gets hurt, then it's a sporting injury.

The best way to end the game is by winning.

If it isn't about winning or losing, how do you decide who played better?

Nice guys finish last.

If we don't throw it, they can't hit it, and we win.

Sex is the only sport that's never cancelled because of bad weather.

If you can't imitate him, don't copy him.

You can still run, even if you jiggle when you jog.

Good sports are seldom good at sports.

It's easy to be a Monday morning expert on what the team should have done over the weekend.

Boxers are blessed with the ability to beat others up.

It's not sporting to pick up lost golf balls while they're still rolling.

They called it golf because all the other four-letter words were taken.

Spectators at a cricket match are known as idiots.

Football is violence on the field, followed by press conferences off the field.

Jumping to conclusions is one of the most popular sports in the world.

But I do exercise, I dodge responsibility and run down the boss.

The only reason I took up jogging was to hear heavy breathing again.

If God had intended women to jog, the streets would have been littered with diamonds.

The similarities in sport are different.

If you can still walk, you can run.

Diamonds are forever, but oranges are for half time.

Digging for facts is better than jumping to conclusions.

A good loser imitates the behaviour of winners.

He's fit, he lies down on the job and sidesteps responsibility.

Sport doesn't build character, it merely reveals it.

Travel

When the brochure says, *minutes from the beach*, it means by air.

Go now. Pisa is leaning, Venice is sinking and the Eiffel Tower is rusting away.

If you look like your passport photo, you're not well enough to travel.

I spoke French in France, but it seems they don't understand their own language.

It's a small world once you've made the long trip to the airport.

Travel makes you feel like you're getting somewhere.

Getting there is half the fun.

Travel is ninety percent anticipation and ten percent recollection.

Travel is a great route every time.

I don't go overseas to feel at home.

There are only two types of travel, first class and with children.

Regardless of which side you're on, the view on the other side is better.

The world is full of cheap tourist destinations, but it's expensive to get to them.

Tourists are terrorists with cameras, terrorists are tourists with guns.

Air travel is being suspended between the illusion of immortality and the reality of death.

If you look like your passport photo, you definitely need a holiday.

If God had intended us to fly economy class, he would have made us much smaller.

If it's Tuesday, it must be Belgium.

A pleasant companion reduces the length of the journey.

Breakfast in London, lunch in New York, luggage in Montreal.

Never try to stay where they don't want you.

The traveller who had a wonderful time created his destination in his mind.

Foreigners always spell better than they pronounce.

Tour guides always visit twenty souvenir shops and one restroom.

A wise traveller never despises his own country.

Always be polite to airline staff. You think it's a coincidence that you go to Sydney and your luggage goes to Melbourne?

Getting there is only half as far as getting there and back.

I have seen more than I remember, and I remember more than I saw.

The more I see of other countries, the more I love my own.

The heaviest luggage is an empty purse.

Travel makes a wise man better and a fool worse.

He who would travel happily must travel light.

Easter is when the council closes the roads and opens all the detours.

Business is so bad that some hotels are stealing the towels back from the guests.

If you're going away, take half as many clothes and twice as much money.

Travel broadens the mind and places a tremendous strain on the bowel.

It's worth seeing, but not worth going to see.

Unusual travel arrangements are intricate dance steps for unseasoned travellers.

If God had intended for us to fly, he would have given us an inbuilt, automatically-activated courage button.

You can have lunch in London, and get your indigestion in New York.

Fly now, pay later.

A police helicopter does not support the theory that pigs can fly.

Travelling with the family is home in motion.

Love

Absence

Kilroy was here, but his spray can was empty.

The eye that isn't focussed on you, is already roaming.

You're always present in my absence.

If we can't be together, keep me in your heart.

Absence is the darkroom where lovers develop negatives.

John absent is still John.

I'm going now, but wait for me in case I get back before I return.

Presents endear absents.

The longest absence is preferable to the longest presence.

I dote on your absence.

Dogs that bark from a distance seldom bite.

The absent grow further away each day.

It takes time for the absent to assume their true shape in our thoughts.

Seldom seen, soon forgotten.

Far from eye, far from heart.

The cure for love is absence.

Where you used to be, there is a hole in the world.

Every degree of separation is a degree of alienation.

The absent have a ringing in the ears when they are talked about.

Distance magnifies the qualities of those we care for.

He who praises you when present, abuses you when absent.

Your absence is good company.

You won't get the part if you don't show up for the audition.

Absent in body, but present in spirit.

It's always the person who is away who made the mistake.

What the eye does not see, the mind does not crave.

Absence is to love what wind is to fire.

I don't mind the separation, but I hate saying goodbye.

Wish you were here, glad you're not.

Long absent, soon forgotten.

My spirit watches over you, even when we are apart.

A short absence increases love at second sight.

Absence sharpens love, presence strengthens it.

Sometimes a day away feels like a month in the country.

Sometimes the best presence of mind is absence of body.

Greater things are believed of those who are absent.

Parting is such sweet sorrow, but not for us.

No-one is indispensable.

In every parting, there is the allusion of death.

The one who is absent will not be declared the heir.

Those who are absent are always in the wrong.

Distance has the same effect on both the heart and the eye.

Absence has a good influence on love.

Absence makes the heart grow fonder, unless it's a case of out of sight, out of mind.

Jealousy

I want the life she's got.

Take away togetherness, and Cupid turns vindictive.

Jealousy creates what it suspects.

The eyes are not responsible when the mind does the seeing.

Don't covet more than you can carry.

You can't expect the turkey to share the enthusiasm of Christmas.

People with strong suspicions have weak minds.

Within every ounce of criticism lies a ton of jealousy.

There is more vanity in jealousy than there is love.

Cupid is a vindictive little bastard.

Jealousy creates its own suspicions.

I'm not weak, I have a strong imagination.

Nothing reveals the smallness of the soul like jealousy does.

Jealousy provides the mud that failure throws at success.

Jealousy stops us from speaking fluently, and makes us think irrationally.

It's not as if I enjoy someone else's suffering, but this is great.

What the eye cannot see, the mind can exaggerate.

Jealousy is a green eyed monster that lives on the love it destroys.

I first desired, but now I want to possess.

Jealous ears misinterpret what they hear.

Jealousy occurs when the second party, the object of affection, engages in an ownership dispute with the first party.

People only throw stones at trees laden with fruit.

Jealousy is the hell where an absent lover lives.

Love creates its own past, the shorter its history.

I might as well, since you already think I do.

Jealousy lives on doubt, and certainty transforms it into fury.

Jealousy is distrust pointed away from itself.

Ashes smother the flame.

Jealousy is the insane desire to keep what doesn't belong to you anyway.

An unfaithful lover makes a jealous husband.

If jealousy was a fever, half the world would be ill.

Jealousy rises in proportion to desire.

Jealousy shuts one door and opens two others.

If I'm capable of deceit, so are you.

Jealousy is an infection of love.

For each one who pities our misfortune, there are a thousand who envy our success.

Jealousy never rests.

Why shouldn't you be jealous of what others have, what else is there to be jealous of?

Jealousy is the suspicion that the person you love is too good for you.

Jealousy is love's green-eyed monster.

To love is to suffer, to be loved is to cause suffering.

Grasp the shadow and lose the substance.

Out of sight, in someone else's arms.

Jealousy devours love.

Admiration and envy are close relatives.

Love

Love may be blind, but it seems to find it's way around.

Love is the triumph of imagination over intelligence.

I fell in love with the face, and ended up married to the mouth.

Love is two minds without a single thought.

If you don't make me happy, I'll make you suffer.

Love is a temporary insanity, curable by marriage.

Love is not gazing at each other, but looking outward together in the same direction.

Hearts split in heaven, and sometimes the two halves find each other on earth.

Sex alleviates the tension that love causes.

Love is the sexual excitement of the young, and the mutual dependence of the old.

Love is the delusion that one man differs from another.

True love is a ghost that everyone talks about, but nobody has seen.

Love doesn't make the world go round, but it makes the trip worthwhile.

When two hearts meet and react to one another, both are transformed.

The perfect pillow on which to rest my head is the one next to yours.

Love needs love to grow on, unless you're a stalker.

It's crazier to be constantly infatuated than to abandon yourself to love just once.

If I was sure you loved me, I could bear to wonder whether I loved you.

Love means never having to admit you're ugly.

Love laughs at locksmiths.

Love isn't blind, it chooses not to see.

Love makes time pass, time makes love pass.

I worship the ground your father discovered oil on.

No man knows the value of a woman's love until he starts paying alimony.

When we feel unloved, we concentrate on our own faults.

When love dies, the ex's faults are magnified.

Love me little, but love me long.

Love is a perpetual wound.

Love is chemistry, sex is physics.

I ache to hold you, or maybe it's just rheumatism.

No-one acts more foolishly than a wise man in love.

When love goes out the door, indifference comes in the window.

Love begins with a fever and ends with a yawn.

An engaged man is a lion, a married man is a puppy dog.

Her feelings for me had changed, but she still loved the ring too much to give it back.

Try to be reasonable about love, and you lose your reason.

Love sees through a telescope, hatred sees through a microscope.

To love is to admire with the heart, to admire is to love with the mind.

Love makes a hard heart tender.

True love is a ghost that everyone talks about, but nobody has seen.

If you're drunk with love, marriage will soon sober you up.

True love is a single soul living in two bodies.

The love you give away always comes back to you.

Love makes the world go around, but money greases its wheels.

Love is the mind overcome by the heart.

The greatest love you can give is when you surrender your soul.

Romance

Don't let a woman beguile you with her shape, it's your barn she's after.

Romance is attraction stimulated by imagination.

Romance is love before being imprisoned in the domestic setting which kills it.

You're perfect, don't ever change. I want to forget you exactly as you are tonight.

See you again? I'd rather go blind.

I've kissed so many girls I could do it with my eyes closed.

I'd love to go out with you, but I have to spend some quality time with myself.

You have to kiss a lot of frogs before you meet the handsome prince.

Being jilted is when the wedding goes off without a hitch.

If we can't be honest with one another, let's lie together.

You need someone to love while you're looking for someone to love.

I had a wonderful evening, but this wasn't it.

If love is blind, how come most people are attracted to beautiful people?

She turned out to be just another near Mrs.

Excuse me, I'm a stranger here, can you direct me to your home?

You were the whole world to me once, but since then I've learned geography.

Romance is a one-night stand that has passed its use-by date.

No, I can't go out with you, I'm expecting a headache.

Flirting is an expression of desire under consideration.

Whoever named it necking was a poor judge of anatomy.

I looked up and there you were, the closest thing to heaven.

Blind dates always look better over the telephone.

The sweetest romance always ends with the bitterest disappointment.

Laugh and the world laughs with you. Snore and you sleep alone.

Love begins in the mind, not the genitals.

Every time I ask for her telephone number, she gives me a dial tone.

She was on the rebound and he was the last resort.

Come behind the pyramid, and I'll make you a mummy.

Weak and willing, provided you meet the right villain.

Don't moan about lost love, it was never wasted.

The most romantic setting has a diamond in it.

I've lost my telephone number. Can I borrow yours?

All I'll ever need apart apart from you, is tremendous self control.

Hot love is soon cold.

If you weren't drop dead gorgeous, you'd be easy to ignore.

When two people fall in love, one usually climbs out alone.

Love at first sight ends at first slight.

Sex without love is just another bodily function.

Romance is where Cupid meets Stupid.

I'd like to see you again, and again and again.

One deceiving, the other believing.

A kiss is a contraction of the mouth due to the enlargement of the heart.

Every Jack has a Jill, or a Jack.

Love is blind, which is why men have to feel their way around.

I chase those who run from me, and run from those who chase me.

I finally found the perfect man, but he had already found the perfect woman.

Marriage

Marriage

Wilt! Thou take this woman to be thy lawful wedded wife?

Marriage is just another union that defies management.

Marriage is everyone's souvenir of love.

Long after the glow has gone, the worm remains.

Marriages are made in heaven, where thunder and lightning come from.

When the beautiful music stops, the strings are still attached.

Holy acrimony.

A second marriage is the triumph of hope over experience.

Let's stay together and drag each other down.

Marriage is where love goes when it gets sick.

It's when you give up the attention of several different men so that you can be ignored by one.

I never knew what happiness was until I got married, but by then it was too late.

Married men live longer, but they are more willing to die.

Marriage isn't a lottery. In a lottery, you at least have a chance.

To marry once is duty, twice is stupidity, and three times is sheer lunacy.

Marriage is like mustard, you praise it with tears in your eyes.

In the small circle of a wedding ring, lies more misery than most people can imagine.

Marriage is the only war where you sleep with the enemy.

Marriage is one long conversation, interrupted by silent disputes.

A bachelor is someone who never makes the same mistake twice.

Marriage is when the housekeeper thinks she's actually a family member.

Marriages might be made in heaven, but you have to live them on earth.

Happily married - she's married, he's happy.

No matter how much cats fight, there are always plenty of kittens.

Marriage is a great institution, but who wants to be institutionalised?

Marriage is a romance in which the hero dies in the first chapter.

A wedding is a funeral where you smell your own flowers.

The money once spent on flowers and restaurants is now spent on supermarkets.

Marriage is a feast, where the grace is better than the meal.

May *For better or Worse* be better than worse.

Marriage is a three ring circus, engagement ring, wedding ring and suffering.

All weddings are happy, it's what happens afterwards that's the problem.

Keep your eyes open before marriage and shut them after.

There's more to marriage than four legs in a bed.

One part love, two parts blindness and one part forgiveness.

Wedlock, padlock.

Bigamy is when two rites make a wrong.

Two can live as cheaply as one, as long as one doesn't eat.

Love is the dawn of marriage, and marriage is the sunset of love.

Marry in haste, repent at leisure.

Marriage is a public confession of a private intention.

Those outside are desperate to get in, and those inside are trying to get out.

Marriage is the only life sentence where you get out early for bad behaviour.

The honeymoon is the period of doting between dating and debating.

Husbands

Some married-looking men are merely worried.

Stalemate.

She was a fool when she married him, but he was in love and he didn't notice.

A tea towel will wipe that contented look off his face.

He rules the roost, and she rules the rooster.

I'm the boss, but I allow my wife to make all our decisions.

Monotony is having only one wife.

I proposed to a goddess, and ended up married to a housewife.

Conquest, request, inquest.

Like a coin, you can't face each other, and yet you're stuck together.

Don't torture yourself, that's my job.

I put a ring on her finger, and she put one through my nose.

What began as a passion ended up as a boring old habit.

Behind every successful man stands a wife with nothing to wear.

The only thing you learn from arguing with your wife is how to be a good loser.

He's been happily married for ten years now, although it has taken him three marriages to get that far.

I now have the maximum of temptation along with the minimum of opportunity.

I can only please one person a day, and today isn't your turn.

A husband may not be the wife's natural enemy, but his lawyer is.

The size of the bouquet is proportionate to the severity of the offence.

I miss my wife's cooking, as often as I can.

I take her everywhere with me, but that's so that I don't have to kiss her goodbye.

Give a husband enough rope, and he'll skip.

I wish I had half as much fun as my wife thinks I do when I'm away on business.

A husband can be too tired to help around the house, yet play eighteen holes of golf.

I wear the pants, but she decides which pair.

If a husband is continually in hot water, he becomes hardboiled.

A husband should tell his wife everything, but only if he thinks there's a chance she might find out anyway.

A husband is the guy in the bar who smiled back once too often.

He's every woman's first husband.

A man who buys his wife two hundred dollar plates will never be allowed to wash up.

Not all men are stupid. Look how many bachelors there are.

I'm the boss, and I have my wife's permission to say so.

The decision to marry was his last independent decision.

He never forgets the wedding anniversary, but he can't remember why he got married.

Never above you, never below you, always beside you. As if.

A husband is what's left of a lover after the name has been extracted.

When he wants cold beer, she sits on the esky.

A husband never has to ask for advice, it's freely available.

An unhappy husband will knowingly drink the poison his wife puts in his tea.

You're right, I don't deserve you. And yet I have constipation, which I don't deserve either.

Only a newly married man tells his wife everything.

The upkeep of a wife is the downfall of a husband.

Wives

Attila the Hen.

Darling is the wife's maiden name.

That argument he thinks he just won, isn't over yet.

The bitter half.

The man I married has become one of my children.

Some wives aren't suspicious, they just know.

If her intuition is so good, how come she has to ask where he's been until three am?

I would rather be right than reasonable.

I waited for the right man to come along, but in the interim, I got married.

A wife is a young man's lover, a middle aged man's companion, and an old man's nurse.

If I play second fiddle, we have domestic harmony.

A wife loves out of duty, duty causes restraint, and constraint kills desire.

A wife is like a tea bag, you never know how strong it is until it gets into hot water.

If it wasn't for his drinking, he would have left her long ago.

It should be a happy marriage, they're both so much in love with her.

I wouldn't act like an old nag if you treated me like a thoroughbred.

Better a rich man's darling than a poor man's slave.

A bride puts her foot down as soon as she crosses the threshold.

First she knits, then she needles.

When she whispers in his ear, she wants something. When she shouts, she didn't get it.

That famous woman's intuition is simply inherent suspicion.

Sometimes I wake up Grumpy, and sometimes I just let him sleep.

Eavesdropping does the work, and intuition gets the credit.

A wife is most attentive when her husband talks in his sleep.

Choose a wife by ear and not by eye.

She began by blocking advances, and ended up blocking retreat.

He that speaks ill of his wife dishonours himself.

She speaks a hundred and forty words a minute, with gusts of up to a hundred and sixty.

I wish she was my mother, so I could run away from home.

She's an angel, always harping on about something or another.

A wife is someone who sticks with you through all the troubles you wouldn't have had if you hadn't married her in the first place.

She feeds him a consistent diet of cold shoulder and hot tongue.

Love was so much better before we married.

Every time she looks in the mirror, she sees the boss.

The most remarkable thing about some women is their husbands.

Kissing doesn't last, good cooking does.

Housekeeping is like stringing beads, without a knot at the end of the thread.

Purse strings are the most common ties.

It was a beautiful dream, but when she woke up, her coffee was cold.

I hate people who drop in unexpectedly and find the house a mess, like it usually is if no-one is supposed to be coming over.

Make time to love me, or someone else will.

Always consider the possibility that he might be right, before discarding the idea as ridiculous.

A woman tries her luck, a man risks his.

In-Laws

The only thing my mother-in-law doesn't know, is why her daughter married me.

Nothing for me, Lord, but my parents so badly want a son-in-law.

A mother-in-law is the beard on the matrimonial oyster.

God made Adam first, because he didn't want Eve's mother issuing instructions over his shoulder.

I like my wife's mother-in-law much better than I like mine.

A mother-in-law is just like a mother, except you hate her.

He married the devil's daughter and moved in with the in-laws.

Interfering is the in-laws loving way of saying you don't know how to raise their grandchildren.

Happiness is a loving mother-in-law, who lives far away.

I haven't spoken to my mother-in-law for months because I don't dare interrupt her.

A mother cries at her daughter's wedding because she's watching her child make the same mistake she made.

My mother-in-law converted me, before I met her I never believed in hell.

It wouldn't hurt to be nice to her, but I don't have a a high threshold of pain.

The son-in-law also rises, but late.

Me, the woman I love, the in-laws and the wedding ring, a vicious circle.

It's only after the wedding that you notice how horribly alike your wife and her mother are.

A mother-in-law is the most common cause of all diseases.

A man is never as bright as his mother thinks he is, or as stupid as his mother-in-law says he is.

My mother-in-law thinks I'm effeminate. Compared to her, I am.

If you must go against your better judgement, do it when she's not around.

He's a terrible son-in-law, but he makes beautiful babies.

Why are there no father-in-law jokes?

A guilty conscience is like a mother-in-law whose visit is eternal.

A man is never as bright as his mother thinks he is, or as stupid as his mother-in-law says he is.

Love was blind, but my mother-in-law restored my sight.

I think she was expelled from the Mafia for cruelty.

I never forget a face, but in my mother-in-law's case I'm willing to make an exception.

When arguing with your mother-in-law, make absolutely certain of your facts before dropping the matter.

I know my mother-in-law can't hurt me, and yet I'm still afraid of her.

It's rude for a man to fall asleep while his mother-in-law is talking, but he has to sleep sometime.

Arguing with your mother-in-law is like starting a war, you can't win it and it's not easy to stop.

Anything he says after she's had the last word is the beginning of a new argument.

The views expressed by the mother-in-law are necessarily those of the management, his wife.

Never insult your mother-in-law publicly, do it in the privacy of your own home.

Divorce

Marriage is the sole cause of divorce.

Alimony is the ransom a happy man pays the devil.

You can have the skunk, but I intend to keep the mink.

An ex-wife is forever.

Marriage wasn't a word, it was a sentence.

The word alimony is derived from Latin, meaning *all his money*.

Paying alimony is like buying oats for a dead horse.

Better to take the tooth out than to live with the constant ache.

Someone who refuses to fight back is called a divorcee.

It was very romantic. She got divorced in the same dress her mother was divorced in.

The only thing divorce proves is whose mother was right in the first place.

I knew her before she knew where her next husband was coming from.

The only legitimate grounds for divorce is marriage.

Alimony is the screwing you get for the screwing you got.

When we were married, I never had sex nearly as often as you did.

He took her for better or worse. She took him for everything.

It's alright to miss your ex-wife as long as your aim is improving.

It began with sentiment and ended with settlement.

A second wife is no cheaper than the first one was.

Ask yourself, is this the man I want my children to spend their weekends with?

He can't fool her, she knows her carats.

The antiquity of marriage precedes divorce by a matter of days.

It's when a romance that began on a sandy beach ends up on the rocks.

He used to kiss the cat and put the wife out.

He tried to sue the priest for malpractice.

She married something that didn't agree with her.

She never hated any man enough to give his diamonds back.

Divorcees remarry because they can stand only so much happiness.

Some divorces are so amicable that the couples remarry.

They didn't even have enough left in common to fight about.

Divorce was the only thing they could agree on.

The latest Barbie doll is Divorce Barbie, who comes with all of Ken's things.

They said I do, but they didn't.

Divorce happens when the father runs away from home instead of the children.

Divorce is the high cost of leaving.

He was loving another man's wife when he should have been loving his own.

Liberty makes a better husband than lost love.

Divorce is difficult for a man. No-one likes to lose a servant.

He never remembered her birthday, but he never forgot how old she was.

He got a divorce two years ago, but he hasn't been game to tell his wife yet.

Alimony is when a man and a woman make a mistake, and the man pays for it.

I would divorce him if I didn't think it would make him incredibly happy.

After divorce, most women feel like a new man.

No man appreciates the value of his wife until he starts paying maintenance.

Baby Bear was from a previous marriage.

Media

Facts

Facts rely on perception.

A fact is a lie with information added to make it more believable.

Get your facts straight first, and then you can panic.

Facts don't disappear just because they're ignored.

You should never allow the facts to stand in the way of the truth.

Get your facts straight first, then you can distort them as much as you like.

Prejudice is a refusal to be confused by facts.

For your information, I would like to ask a question.

There are no facts, only interpretations.

The little facts that are undermined today, are the foundation for tomorrow's big truths.

You have to read between the lies.

Never assume the obvious is true.

The more you run over a dead cat, the flatter it gets.

Accept the fact that you live in a world of illusion.

Blessed are the flexible, for they shall not be bent out of shape.

My mind is made up. Don't confuse me with facts.

It must be true, I saw it on television.

We don't need all the facts to bring you all the details.

It's not that they lie, they just live on the wrong side of the facts.

Give me the facts and I will draw my own confusions.

Newspapers and current affairs shows are the natural enemies of facts.

The hand that controls the media controls the country.

To start a riot, just rub two opposing views together.

It's not an optical illusion, it just looks that way.

A censor is someone who knows more than he thinks you ought to.

My story may have changed, but not the fact that I'm never wrong.

The editor's truth is more important than your facts.

Getting at the truth is like hacking your way through a forest with a feather.

We don't really want information unless it corroborates our opinion.

If you're not confused, you're not paying attention.

Facts only confuse a clear cut issue.

Some facts exist merely to be ignored.

The information we get merely confirms the editor's opinion.

The more facts you have, the harder it becomes to form an opinion.

There are no eternal facts.

An editor is indebted to his imagination for his facts.

Freedom of the press is the privilege only of those who own the press.

Anything is possible if you don't know what you're talking about.

If facts threaten to spoil an otherwise good story, omit them.

News expands to fill the time and space allotted for its coverage.

When you're right, no-one remembers. When you're wrong, no-one forgets.

The media deducts fact from hypothesis, and publishes the outcome.

An editorial is a minimum number of facts, combined with prejudice and emotion.

The editorial condemns gambling and the sports section prints racing tips.

Journalism

If it bleeds, it leads.

We can endure anything, except someone else's wealth and power.

Publish and be damned. And they did, and he was.

When the media refers to someone as venerable, it means he's so old he should be dead, but for some reason, isn't.

Reporters are parasites who live off other people's misery.

Hero today, gone tomorrow.

Journalists work harder than most other lazy people.

One man's news is another man's sorrow.

Journalism keeps us in touch with the ignorance of the community.

The news is always the same, it just happens to different people.

The best story starts with an earthquake and builds its way up to a climax.

Most journalists don't know the difference between creative writing and reporting.

Is the world getting worse, or are reporters merely working harder?

Journalism is the area between factual reporting and creative writing.

Journalism is the artistic integration of fact and fiction.

Controversial means someone did something the media can't prove.

There's always room for the retraction, but not on the front page where the erroneous information was originally printed.

The windows to other worlds are covered with newspaper.

Television will never replace newspapers because you can't swat a fly with a television set.

If the editor can make the people angry enough, they will write the editorial for him.

From the sublime to the ridiculous is a single step.

Journalism has enhanced the spread of mass illiteracy.

Freedom of the press is when an editor prints a dictator's speech, but didn't have to.

Journalism is literature's performing flea.

When smashing monuments, keep the pedestals, they come in handy.

When it's far away, it's a tragedy. At home, it's news.

I'll publish right or wrong. Fools are my theme, satire is my song.

Never offend people with style if you can offend them with substance.

Man arrested for possession of heroine.

Journalistic integrity is a matter of whose side you are on.

Begin with something so simple that it hardly seems worth stating, and end with something so paradoxical that no-one will believe it.

Any informant who never produces misinformation is too deviant to be trusted.

A newspaper is a big disaster on the front page with more bad news inside.

Journalists are writers who didn't make the grade.

Today Snow White would be described as a nymphomaniac living with seven vertically challenged miners who destroyed a rain forest.

Newspapers are dead trees with information smeared over them.

The editor's opinion dictates the errors and omissions.

I am in favour of freedom of the press, provided it's kept under rigid control.

No wonder sportsmen punch photographers. How would you like your every failure published on the front page?

Newspapers are useful for preventing paint splashes on floors.

Public Opinion

Public opinion is what people think people think.

You can fool all the people some of the time, and some of the people all of the time.

Public opinion is the result of numerous editorials.

If fifty million people believe a foolish thing, it is still a foolish thing.

We are mushrooms. They keep us in the dark and feed us bullshit.

The audience that hissed yesterday may applaud for the same performance today.

Public opinion is the view of the minority, expressed as the views of the majority.

The media exists to widen our scope of worry.

We are governed by what the press allows us to know.

The editor's opinion soon becomes the public's principle.

Study the newspaper, and you will be extremely well informed as to the editor's opinion.

Right is right, even if everyone is against it.

Public opinion is the nonsense of editorial opinion.

When you find yourself on the side of the majority, pause and reflect.

We live under the protection of our own cowardice, which we call principle.

It's easier to point a finger than it is to offer a helping hand.

Truth is not determined by majority vote.

If you can't change your mind, you can't change anything.

We can participate in public opinion without the inconvenience of having to think for ourselves.

Public opinion is an editor's viewpoint intended to make life uncomfortable for anybody who isn't content to be a nobody.

It's easier to believe a lie you've heard a thousand times before, than a truth you've never heard before.

Four hostile newspapers are to be feared more than a thousand bayonets.

The world is governed more by public opinion than by morality.

Public opinion is a newspaper article that attracted attention.

Men are easy to convince that what they already believe is true.

Journalism used to be current history, but it's degenerated into unsubstantiated gossip.

Assassination is the most extreme form of censorship.

We confuse the headlines with public opinion.

Everybody favours free speech when they have no axe to grind.

Public opinion is what the media tell us the majority of people think.

Public opinion has more control over public figures than morality does.

For your information, I would like to ask a question.

What's fit to print isn't necessarily fit to read.

What bothers the editor will ultimately bother the whole country.

Public opinion is prejudiced gossip exaggerated by media.

Much outcry, little result.

Embattled means the media is about to prove he's guilty.

An informed source is anyone who volunteered information.

Freedom of the press spreads propaganda.

Publish it, or perish it.

The essence of belief is the establishment of habit.

Credulity is the man's weakness and the child's strength.

Prejudice

Bigotry

When are you going to eat pork, Rabbi Levi? At your wedding, Father O'Reilly.

The narrower the mind, the broader the prejudice.

So careful of the type, so careless of the life.

We are all equal, but some are more equal than others.

You are the inferior of any person whose rights you trample underfoot.

A bigot is a person who slams his mind in your face.

A bigot reaches the same conclusion his father did, with an equal lack of thought.

Any man's death diminishes me, for I am involved in mankind.

Intolerance is the last defence of the insecure.

If you're not prejudiced, people think you don't understand the social system.

You can't hold someone down without staying down with him.

If I am not for others, who will be for me?

What we really need is more of them and fewer of us.

Illegal aliens have always been a problem, ask any Aboriginal.

A crucifix? Oi vey, have you got the wrong vampire.

To denounce prejudice, is prejudice itself.

Jesus was Jewish, but only on his mother's side.

There is no they, only us.

The Jewish Mafia, Kosher Nostra.

Equality can be decreed by law, but it cannot be enforced by law.

Doubt is directed more against the accuser within than the assailant without.

Ignorance is forgivable, but prejudice never.

How odd of God to choose the Jews.

Nothing crushes a new idea faster than a narrow mind.

We overcome what we assimilate.

A rabbi? What kind of job is that for a nice Jewish boy?

Bigotry grips truth so tightly that it suffocates it.

Everyone is entitled to his own opinion, as long as it coincides with the minority viewpoint.

Affirmative action is prejudice wearing its other outfit.

Anti-Semitism is the Gentile art of making enemies.

Those who believe absurdities, commit atrocities.

Some people are so narrow minded that they have to stack their prejudices vertically.

The arrogant exist above equality, looking down with nastiness.

Bigotry is the certainty about something we know nothing about.

Jews are just like everyone else, only more so.

A bigot is someone who is too stubborn to admit I'm right.

The mind of a bigot contracts when light shines on it.

It's easy to see both sides of the question as long as your prejudices aren't involved.

Because prejudice isn't based on reason, it can't be resolved by debate.

There are two ways of doing this, my way and the wrong way.

Everyone's quick to blame the foreigner.

No man is no better than his prejudices.

When you find out you're nobody, you find out everyone else is too.

Racism

What makes equality difficult is that everyone only wants to be equal with their superiors.

I've seen God. She's black.

We're all Adam's children, but some sat in the sun and some sat in the shade.

Those that don't form part of the top fifty percent, form part of the bottom fifty percent.

The ignorant are always prejudiced and the prejudiced are always ignorant.

I'm an equal opportunity bigot, I dislike everyone equally.

Neo-nazis are a national affront.

Don't pack your prejudice if you emigrate.

A man's colour makes him no better or worse a person than he already is.

It's difficult to explain to white mice that black cats are lucky.

Racial prejudice is a vagrant opinion with no visible means of support.

There is no cure for the blind in mind.

Racism makes the world unsafe for diversity.

He's not a racist, he doesn't care what colour his slaves are.

Friends come in various shades of skin.

You can't argue with racism, because it isn't based on logic.

The tears of a stranger are only water.

The difference between a conviction and a prejudice is that you can defend a conviction rationally.

All men are born different but equal.

I don't care what colour your skin is, it's your attitude that bothers me.

Beware of the man with only one book.

If we were all the same colour, someone would devise another reason for senseless hatred.

Instead of pretending not to notice each other's differences, why don't we celebrate them?

He who never leaves his own country is full of prejudice.

Prejudice is opinion based on hatred.

White does not neutralise black, nor does black neutralise white.

All blood is red.

A good horse cannot be a bad colour.

Racial prejudice is when you condemn the accused without waiting for the verdict.

Racism is the fire of an overheated mind.

Racism isn't dead, but at least it has a frightened look in its eye.

Whites tan to go brown, and blacks bleach to go white.
Why can't they just meet somewhere in the middle?

Live like brothers or die like animals.

Racism is the snobbery of the inferior.

Affirmative action: two wrongs don't make a right.

It's never too late to give up your prejudices.

A whole race gets the credit for a small group's behaviour.

I have a headache, and my prejudice is swollen.

Racism is dying, but the funeral procession goes on and on.

If God hadn't wanted us to be prejudiced, he would have made us all the same colour.

Can't you recognise a sob unless it sounds the same as yours?

Snobbery

Let them eat Corgi.

The upper crust is a lot of crumbs sticking together.

A cauliflower is a cabbage with a college education.

The higher a monkey climbs, the more you can see of its butt.

Who can refute a sneer?

Everybody is entitled to my opinion.

The toes you step on today might belong to the arse you have to kiss tomorrow.

Conceit isn't so bad when the right sort of people have it.

When in doubt, use clout.

I talk to myself because I enjoy talking to a better class of person.

A snob can cut you dead quicker than an autopsy can.

Money is still the most efficient labour saving device.

If we start letting them in, before you know it, there won't be anyone left to look down on.

A snob is not content to be what he appears to be.

Once the game is over, the king and the pawn both go back in the same box.

In a cemetery, wealth is exhibited by the size of the headstone, but nobody cares.

Please check again, my name must be there.

I wouldn't want to belong to a club that would have me as a member.

If the poor want dinner, why don't they just ring the dinner bell?

Our dog's pedigree is so outstanding that, even if he could talk, he wouldn't talk to you.

Nothing will content him who is not content with little.

Better to stand tall in the dust than to crawl on your belly near the throne.

A bore seeks revenge for his own lack of lustre by inflicting his attention on his betters.

Every slum has its own aristocracy.

Good breeding is the ability to conceal our high opinion of ourselves and our low opinion of others.

When I want your opinion, I'll give it to you.

The penalty of success is to be bored by people who once snubbed you.

A throne is just a fancy chair.

How dare you, do you know who I am?

A lion is ashamed to hunt with a fox.

If you want to know how high up you've become, just look down.

But my secretary made the appointment weeks ago.

If it wasn't for good breeding, intimacy would degenerate into coarse familiarity.

The bottom is still the bottom even if it's turned upside down.

Every frog is a prince in disguise.

Status symbols are medals you buy yourself.

A sparrow pities a peacock for the burden of its tail.

When I hear the word gun, I reach for my culture.

All the people like us are *We,* and everyone else is *They.*

Culture is something grown in a glass dish in a laboratory.

A fly that sits on a king's head is still just a fly.

Everyone agrees that there are no social superiors, but few deny they have social inferiors.

We only use Perrier, even in the spa.

Snobs have no class and their neighbours are conscious of it.

Progress

Computers

User error. Replace user and press any key to continue.

Do windows really need gates?

If God had meant us to use computers, he would have given us more patience.

Feeling lucky, punk? Go on, update your software.

Artificial intelligence is no substitute for natural stupidity.

On the keyboard of life, always keep your finger on the escape button.

It's really very simple, a mouse is an electrical gadget that you point at an icon to open a file so that you can retrieve an item.

That's not a bug, it's a feature.

It's not the size of your hard drive that counts, it's the way you download it.

Unified technology equals homogenised humanity.

The information highway condenses the world into a global village.

A computer should never be used without child supervision.

First my hard disc overloaded and then my motherboard fried.

Computers speak Computerese, a language understood mainly by children and a small group of adults.

To continue, pound keyboard with fist.

If it's not on fire, then it's a software problem.

You mean that sliding drawer isn't a cup holder?

We are Microsoft. Resistance is futile. You will be assimilated.

I always knew it was a mistake to let a mechanical object know you're afraid of it.

All computer errors lead back to a human.

Some computers are so advanced that they blame their mistakes on humans.

If you're at home with a computer, you're home alone.

I am logged in, therefore I am.

By the time I mastered the exceptions, I'd forgotten which rules they applied to.

Computers may be unreliable, but humans are even more unreliable.

Computers are nothing new, Eve had an Apple.

Immunity to boredom gives computers the edge over humans.

There is no such thing as electronic privacy.

Just when I got the modified programme to work, they decided to stick with the old one.

When the computers go down, workers wander around dazed, wondering what to do.

As a computer, I find human faith in me astonishing.

By the time you understand the technology, it's obsolete.

The government keeps track of humans through computers.

To err is human, to really stuff it up, it takes a computer.

Computers will never replace human beings until they're programmed to laugh at the boss's jokes.

If it cuts my workload by half, how come I'm so far behind?

Software is what makes your hardware smarter than you are.

Blessed are the pessimists, for they make backups.

Computers are a product of human imagination.

It only lets you win games if someone programmed it to let you win.

We are proud of computers, and suspicious of people who think they can't think.

Environment

Keep it clean, others have to live here after you.

With all the rain we've had recently, if I had a suspicious nature, I'd build an ark.

You know spring has sprung when the smog starts to turn green.

Technology owes ecology an apology.

Don't pray for rain, dam it.

The ratio of acceptable levels of pollution rises in direct proportion to the size of the polluter's last campaign contribution.

We are preceded by forest and followed by desert.

We do not inherit the earth from our ancestors, we borrow it from our descendents.

Breathing may be hazardous to your health.

An avalanche is when the hill comes down the hill.

Take only pictures, and leave nothing but footprints.

Crop circles are cereal killers.

Growth for the sake of growth is the ideology of the cancer cell.

Tickle the earth with a hoe, and she laughs with a harvest.

How many times a decade does the coldest day in thirty years come around?

There is more than enough to satisfy our needs, but not enough to satisfy our greed.

We conquered nature, and now we're beating it to death.

Asthma is proof that we're paying through the nose for air pollution.

With so much air pollution, there would be nowhere to store it all, if it wasn't for our lungs

In countries where nature does the most, men do the least.

India's climate is so severe that its inhabitants have to live elsewhere.

Wouldn't it be ironic if the world ended before we destroyed it?

God made heaven and earth, and man is destroying them.

Man is a user, not a creator.

What's the point of a beautiful house with landscaped gardens, if there's no planet to put it on?

It's not about finding new horizons, it's about looking at existing ones differently.

Why is our water lumpy?

What we destroy today, nature will revenge itself for tomorrow.

The preservation of the world is in the wilderness.

Each age chooses the death it will die.

Artificial inscmination is a lot of bull.

Vesuvius is a volcano and you can see the creator smoking there day and night.

Nature is God's art.

If Moses wanted to part the sea today, he would need a shovel.

Don't laugh, you might inhale the air.

Nature has no malice.

It's so cold that when you open the front door, the lights come on.

An acceptable level of pollution is still pollution.

Pity the meek, for they shall inherit the earth.

A virgin forest is where the hand of man has never set foot.

One day summer, the next day winter.

Nine months winter, with another three cold months in summer.

Technology

In the beginning, there was nothing, and it exploded with a big bang.

Now that we have the technical ability to move mountains, who needs faith?

If it stinks, it's chemistry.

Yesterday's problem is tomorrow's achievement.

Anyone who's ever had a self-cleaning oven knows that it means you have to clean it yourself.

Dishwashers are useless, paper plates clog them up.

Gravity is a farce, the earth sucks.

An active social life can't take place in a computer chat room.

Prisoners in jails are allowed television sets in their cells, as part of their punishment.

A meteorologist can look into a girl's eyes and see whether.

Don't panic, you're supposed to glow like that.

Nuclear waste fades your genes.

The telephone is an instrument of inconvenient convenience.

Earth is the lunatic asylum of the solar system.

Nuclear capability means we can nuke them till they glow, and then shoot them in the dark.

If the world is a global village, how come travel is so expensive?

The first rule of tinkering is to keep all the parts.

Space technology means politicians can now deliver the moon they've been promising.

The world will not end with a bang, but with a whimper.

No machine can do the work of one extraordinary man.

The fruits of victory are ashes in your mouth.

Nuclear power ensures that all men will be cremated equal.

If the formula for water is H2O, is the formula for an ice cube H20 squared?

Tools to him what can handle them.

We have the power to make this the best generation in history, or the last one.

He left his body to science, but science is contesting the will.

I'm a mere clone of my former self.

In research, the most interesting results only occur once.

Technology is dominated by two types, those who understand what they manage, and those who manage what they understand.

If it doesn't work, that's physics.

If it wasn't for Thomas Edison, we'd be watching television by candlelight.

Gravity is getting me down.

Do not look directly into the laser with your remaining eye.

New roads, new ruts.

We are nuclear giants and ethical infants.

Discovery consists of seeing what everyone else has seen, but thinking what no-one else has thought.

The pot calls the kettle electric.

Never force it, get a bigger hammer.

People ridicule science fiction, and yet they believe economists and the weather bureau.

Each age has the choice of death it will die.

Space travel is an extravagant feat of technological exhibitionism.

We are the slaves or our own labour saving devices.

Religion

God

If you want to make God laugh, tell him your plans.

We all believe in God, but some of us spell his name differently.

God enters the soul through the cracks in a broken heart.

Maybe God's motives aren't so noble, maybe he just kills us for fun.

If what the bible says is true, can man ever find it in his heart to forgive God?

How can I make my peace with God when we have never quarrelled?

Oh Lord, if there is a Lord, save my soul, if I have a soul.

God is slow, but he always pays in full.

God will never allow anything to happen to you that he doesn't think he can handle.

Pray to God, but don't let go of the ledge.

God creates, man shapes.

The notion of sin, without a belief in God, is ludicrous.

God is the name of the ultimate generalisation.

Prayer is talking to God, but God help you if you can hear him answer.

God resembles the race worshipping him.

Oh God, thy sea is so great, and my boat is so small.

God is busy, please save yourself.

A dyslexic wonders if there really is a Dog.

God does not need to exist, to save us.

God is an underachiever.

God is a comedian playing to an audience too afraid to laugh.

Perhaps God punishes us because he envies us our mortality.

If this is what it's like when God's on our side, heaven help us if he turns against us.

God isn't dead, he just doesn't want to get involved.

God is alive and well and working on a much less ambitious project.

We fear men so much because they fear God so little.

If God created us in his own image, we have more than reciprocated.

God is not a cosmic room service that can be summoned at will.

Be at peace with God, whatever you perceive him to be.

God gives the milk, but not the jug.

Religion is between man and church. Faith is between man and God.

Only God knows if there is a God.

If God seems far away, who made the first move?

God arrives for inspections without announcing his intention.

God was a woman until she changed her mind.

Thank God I'm an atheist.

If God didn't exist, man would invent him.

If we are all innocent, the concept of God is unthinkable.

God loads the dice.

Everything that happens on a Sunday isn't a work of God.

I know God won't give me anything he thinks I can't handle, but I wish he didn't trust me so much.

An honest God is the noblest work of man.

Never object to religion unless it interferes with God's work.

Clergy

I've been through hell, and I've brought you back religion.

Jesus is coming, look busy.

There's the pope, speak of the devil.

Just because they wear the uniform, doesn't mean they know the boss personally.

Even when you're dying, the priest just has to have the last word.

Heaven won't have me, and hell is afraid I'll take over.

At least sinners don't make a living out of sin like some people do.

Blasphemy is irreverence towards deity.

They can no more ask God the way to heaven than you can.

Priests are the only people who go to church because it's good for business.

Oh Lord, nudge me before I say too much.

So much religion, so little faith.

You may use maths in birth control, but we condemn your use of chemistry.

The eleventh commandment, thou shalt not be found out.

The best places in hell are reserved for the clergy.

I work for the Lord. The pay's great and the benefits are out of this world.

The bible tells us what they should do, newspapers tell us what they actually do.

There is no rogue like a religious rogue.

The clergy are not human Sundays.

The pope doesn't let priests marry because he doesn't want the wives telling everyone what their husbands learned in the confessional.

Make me chaste, dear Lord, but not today.

Not all those who use holy water are saints.

What you put in the collection plate, the priest sends to heaven ahead of you, as a down payment on forgiveness for your sins.

They are only against other's sins.

Where blasphemy is forbidden, atheism thrives.

They would have us believe God has delegated himself to millions of deputies.

A sad demise, eaten by missionaries.

The mouth that prays, also whispers obscenities.

He is often a father to the children of the parish, literally.

Feel superior, become a nun.

He is a man of the cloth, cashmere.

They have to climb over the church to find happiness.

Faith is in the heart, not in the knees.

If they don't play the game, how come they get to make the rules?

There are three sexes: men, women and clergymen.

If you can't be chaste, be careful.

It's easy to be celibate, but only when you're very old.

There should have been another commandment.

Christianity provides a hell for its enemies and a heaven for its friends.

Celibacy is its own punishment.

People who know how to behave never preach.

The sermon was so good the congregation hardly slept a wink.

They're the people who amended the Ten Commandments.

The closer to church, the further from God.

Religion

Church is where you take your clothes for others to see how fine you are.

Confession is Sunday's remorse for Saturday's pleasure.

Religion is based on the fear of the many and the eloquence of the few.

Our church welcomes all denominations, twenties, fifties and hundreds.

Oh Lord, save me from your followers.

If only the Lord would provide until he provides.

Is there life before death?

Religion is man's need for assurance that there is life after life.

If faith can cure cancer, why can't it grow new limbs?

Money doesn't grow on trees, and that's what congregations are for.

Be afraid, because God is just.

There is only one religion, but there are hundreds of versions of it.

Atheism is a non-prophet organisation.

Every saint has a past and every sinner has a future.

If you love God, you must destroy the church.

Worship the gods and heed their words, but never send money.

Religion is a mask which often hides a hideous face.

Christianity is when dogma overrides karma.

The church needs a computer to count their blessings.

Man makes holy what he believes in.

How many people have died for gentle Jesus, meek and mild?

You can do very little with faith, but you can do nothing without it.

A papal bull is a ferocious animal kept by the pope to trample on Protestants.

Where did Cain and Abel find wives?

I would rather have a mind opened by wonder than one closed by faith.

Religion exists to punish those with a greater capacity for happiness than our own.

Faith is the intellectual acceptance of what intuition has already told you.

Welcome to the Church of the Holy Cabbage. Lettuce pray.

Religion is the fashionable substitute for faith.

We pay for blind faith with real cash payments.

Doubt is an element of faith.

Like organised crime, religion preys on the weak, generates huge profits and cannot be eradicated.

The test of a secure religion is whether you can joke about it.

What you are looking for in church, is everywhere.

Catholicism is a spiritual virus.

Miracles are usually learnt about from dead people, who learned it from someone who heard about it from someone who knew someone whose mother it had happened to.

Man doesn't know how to create a worm, and yet he can create gods by the dozen.

Christianity teaches us forgiveness, and eternal damnation in hell.

An atheist is someone who believes that what you see is what you get.

If you go to church regularly you will have a perfect life, but later.

Religious people mysteriously always know exactly what God wants.

No-one with a sense of humour ever founded a religion.

Easter is cancelled. They found the body.

So is Christmas. Joseph was the father after all.

Good

Morality is the mutual suspicion of moral decrepitude.

We always confess everyone else's sins except our own.

Goodness is the decency left over after our cravings have been satisfied.

He who lives in a glass house should never invite over he who is without sin.

No-one is ever completely evil, he can do good by serving as a bad example.

In a cannibal country, cannibalism is moral.

If you don't stand for anything, you fall for everything.

Man is superior to animals in that he knows right from wrong, but it's a downhill trip from there.

Those who talk like angels, live like people.

Guilt is the price God asks of a bad conscience whenever he checks his notebook.

The more ashamed he ought to be, the more respectable he appears to be.

A tithe is when you pay the devil a toll to get into heaven.

God is good, but he doesn't rub your nose in it.

His integrity would fit into the navel of a flea and there would still be room for his heart.

When a widow loudly denies her intention to ever remarry, the wedding to her next husband has already been arranged.

It must be good to be good, otherwise we wouldn't all pretend to be.

We demonstrate our goodness by condemning the badness of others.

There is nothing so bad that it can't masquerade as a moral.

Morality can see evil even where none exists.

Moral indignation is jealousy with a halo.

We forgive a bad deed if the motive was good, but only for ourselves.

Few have the courage to be what they are.

The road to morality is through sin.

When the devil's happy, he's also good.

Goodness doesn't sparkle, it's dull.

Morality is the luxury of those with nothing to lose.

A man is only as good as his word.

Infidels are those whose beliefs differ from our own.

It's the courage to speak and the ability to listen.

Morality is easy if you're ugly and unpopular.

The louder he talked about honesty, the faster we counted the silverware.

You can give and still keep a promise.

The more I get to know people, the less I expect from them.

He that promises much, delivers nothing.

When morality preaches, goodness undoes itself.

If goodness is not in supply, demand diminishes.

Don't seek examples of goodness, be one.

Morality is the awful thought that someone might be enjoying something you don't approve of.

Goodness is easier to recognise than to define.

Morality is expedient.

Morality is the sacrifice others must make to co-operate with society.

Those that appear to be too good to be true, usually are.

Behaviour cannot be determined by law, but by breeding.

Evil

Get thee behind me Satan, and push.

The devil is that nasty inner being that throttles your conscience.

The threat of hell gives heaven the support it needs.

If faith can move mountains, scepticism can deny their existence.

The devil's boots don't creak.

Do unto others as you think they will do unto you, but do it first.

I don't like to commit myself about heaven and hell. I have friends in both places.

Sinners may be evil, but they're rarely lonely.

I'm not greedy, I just want it all.

Better to rule in hell than to serve in heaven.

Churches do not exist to destroy evil, but to supervise it.

There are no interesting people in heaven, because they're all in hell.

The devil is the shark in your goldfish bowl.

We resent small indiscretions, but permit great evils.

The devil is fine, as long as you keep your foot on his neck.

I'm here because the harp and robes were too expensive.

The devil doesn't fear a dusty cross.

Mother's milk nourishes killers as well as heroes.

Maybe earth is another planet's hell.

Between two evils, always try the one you haven't tried before.

Jesus' martyrdom was meaningless if we don't carry on sinning.

The notion of hell will never be relinquished as long as it represents a source of potential income.

The wages of sin depend on what sort of deal you cut with the devil.

The evil that men do lives after them.

Ignore evil, and you become an accomplice.

A good Christian is a Muslim's evil infidel.

Malicious people die, but malice lives on.

Hell is where the motorists are French, the policemen are German, and the cooks are English.

May your stay in hell be as pleasant as the journey there was.

Puritanism is the haunting fear that someone somewhere may be happy.

A necessary evil is the one we can rationalise.

One man's heaven is another man's hell.

One evil flows from another.

Adam and Eve ate themselves out of house and home.

Every time we dial a prayer, there's a busy signal.

The devil's children have the devil's luck.

Evil is carved in rock, goodness is written in water.

Evil excuses itself by saying its motives were good.

God created the world but the devil keeps it going.

Evil makes a crooked path look straight.

The devil seems to be kinder to people than God is.

All evils level out when they become extreme.

All is not right with the world.

Honesty sets limits to power, which evil easily overcomes.

Sexuality

Heterosexuals

To all the virgins out there, thanks for nothing.

Sex is a sleepless struggle.

An honest owl never lies, there have been other pussycats.

It used to watch me brush my teeth, but now it watches me shine my shoes.

A penis is available in three sizes: small, medium, and *Oh my God.*

Don't worry, I had the same problem when I was a man.

Monogamy leaves a lot to be desired.

Take off my dress, now my underwear, and if I ever catch you wearing my things again, there'll be trouble.

Chastity is its own punishment.

A sex symbol is someone whose private relations are public knowledge.

Never accept lifts from strange men, and remember that all men are a little strange.

My father swears blind that contraceptives don't work.

The cost is exorbitant, the pleasure is fleeting, and the position is simply ridiculous.

One plus one equals three or four.

I believe in love at first sight, it saves so much time.

Sex is nobody's business but the three people involved.

A man names his penis because he doesn't like a stranger making his most important decisions for him.

People who live in glass houses are exhibitionists.

Sex is part of nature, and I always go along with nature.

Oh Lord, grant me chastity, but only when I'm very old.

A playboy toys with sex.

A kiss was devised for the mutual stoppage of speech at a moment when words become utterly superfluous.

Impotence is notion without motion.

Never have an affair with anyone you work with, it's like buying your meat from the newsagent.

He dresses well, and quickly too.

Don't ask me about the men in my life, ask me about the life in my men.

He looks good on any woman.

Vasectomy is the unkindest cut of all.

Contraceptives should be used on all conceivable occasions.

Of all the sexual aberrations, chastity is the weirdest.

Was that an earth tremor, or did you actually move?

Virginity, one prick and it's gone.

A fertile mind is no compensation for a vasectomy.

Eunuchs unite, you have nothing to lose.

Never waste an erection, even if you're on your own.

Artificial insemination keeps your hand in.

Sex is alright, but it's not as good as the real thing.

They stayed up all night waiting for their sexual relations to arrive.

Give masochists a fair crack of the whip.

A platonic friendship is the period between the introduction and the first kiss.

Homosexuality

A homosexual is a man who has cheated some poor woman out of alimony.

A lesbian is just another bloody woman who has taken over a man's job.

I'm not a practicing homosexual, this is as good as I get.

Forget it, Sister, he plays for the other team.

Remember the good old days when there were only two sexes?

You don't have to be rich to live like a queen.

He wants to eat, drink and be Mary.

She-male.

Men are getting in touch with their feminine side, women are getting in touch with their masculine side, and gays are confused.

He enjoys the thrill of the hunt, but he doesn't like to keep what he catches.

The only instrument I ever play is the upright organ.

Well, bugger me. With pleasure.

A gay likes his vice versa.

A male quartet has eight legs and flies.

He gets on best with women who know how to get on without men.

Be gay now and avoid being given the bum's rush later.

It takes all sorts to make a sex.

Only one man in a thousand is a leader of men, the rest follow women.

She thought bi-sexuality was being with two women at the same time.

Being gay not only lets you have home cooked meals, but gives you a variety of cooks.

Which of us is the opposite sex?

Never leave two queens alone, they'll redecorate.

Boys will be boys, and apparently so will some girls.

The brain is my second most favourite organ.

Oral sex isn't just talking about it.

No, the tooth fairy is not a gay dentist.

Kilroy was queer.

I don't sleep with whores, at least not knowingly.

He's dedicated to life, liberty and the happiness of pursuit.

John Fitzpatrick and Patrick Fitzjohn.

Lesbian cyclists - dykes on bikes.

A lesbian is a pansy without a stalk.

She's the best man.

Flies spread disease, so keep yours zipped up.

Ashore it's wine, women and song, aboard it's rum, bum and concertina.

Every pair is not a couple.

Married men have better halves, but homosexuals have better quarters.

Mardi Gras - pooftahs on parade.

If horse racing is the sport of kings, then drag racing is the sport of queens.

If my aunt were a man she'd be my uncle.

AC/DC.

Nobody loves a forty year-old fairy.

Homosexuals can't have it both ways.

Homophobia is what a bigot expends condemning what he despises.

Promiscuity

Why buy the cow when you can get the milk for nothing?

Your body is a temple, not an amusement park.

I am always looking for meaningful one night stands.

Do you mind if I bore the pants off you?

When I'm good, I'm very, very good, but when I'm bad, I'm better.

If I'm not in bed by midnight, I'm going home in a pumpkin.

Be sure to write, even if it's only a cheque.

I don't care where you take me, as long as you take me.

When women go wrong, men go right after them.

Lie down, I think I love you.

Sex appeal, please give generously.

Call me mercenary, but call me anytime.

There's no need to get married, take it from me.

Sorry, I didn't mean to wake you.

If you can't be good, be good at it.

If you've got it, flaunt it.

The one you knock back is the one you miss out on.

She went professional when it occurred to her she was sitting on a goldmine.

She could read men like a book, and she liked to read in bed.

Incompatibility: Your income, my 'patability'.

Let's forget about the six feet and talk about the six inches.

Virtue is its own revenge.

Orgasm donor.

A woman's virtue is man's greatest invention.

If you can't be with the one you love, love the one you're with.

I've had several ex-husbands, apart from my own.

To err is human, but it feels divine.

It's not the men in my life that count, it's the life in my men.

She lived in a penthouse until the old louse expired.

When he said she had a beautiful body, she held it against him.

Help wanted. Many positions available.

A great entertainer, but only from the waist down.

VD is nothing to clap about.

A hard man is good to find.

I collect diamonds, it's my hobby.

Quick, pretend you know me.

I can be had.

All cats are grey in the dark.

There's nothing complex about it, anyone can grasp her.

Goodness, what lovely diamonds. Goodness has nothing to do with it.

That fur coat does a lot for her, but then she did a lot for it.

Her conscience never no's what's wrong.

He has a gift for making love, it's cash.

Give me a sixteen year old and I'll turn him twenty five.

If it weren't for orgasms, he wouldn't know when to stop.

You can't make him stay today for what happened last night.

Society

Community

One man's floor is another man's ceiling.

When the head aches, the body hurts.

No them, no us.

The most contented community is filled with homogenised humanity.

No-one can whistle a symphony. It takes an orchestra to play it.

We don't all have to play the same instrument, as long as we all play in the same key.

The same fence that keeps others out, keeps you a prisoner within.

Distance doesn't make you smaller, it just makes you part of the bigger picture.

The quality of individual lives diminishes in direct proportion to the increase in the world population.

There are only two types of people, those who have more dinners than appetite, and those who have more appetite than dinners.

A happy community is one where individuals have traded their own principles for those of the community.

Ants act only for the good of the group, but they are mindless slaves who attack others who dare to stray into their territory.

There is always someone who knows your duty better than you do.

So many humans, so little humanity.

Population can't keep growing like this, where are we going to put them all?

The more humanity advances technically, the further it degrades itself morally.

The trouble with humanity, is humanity.

The happiest community has no outstanding characters.

Farmers are the basis upon which civilisation is based.

The little potatoes are beneath the big potatoes, propping them up.

Practise random acts of beauty and senseless acts of love.

Snowflakes are fragile, yet they achieve much by sticking together.

Civilisation caters to the body at the expense of the mind.

God created the Garden of Eden, but Adam built the city.

Humanity is truth, love and kindness, which exists only on paper.

There's so much to learn from people who see the world differently from what you do.

Humanity is an unbearable pity for the suffering of mankind.

If you seek company, you must serve it too.

I always feel as if I am trespassing in someone else's perfect world.

The average man knows he is above his average neighbours.

Man is the only animal that blushes, and the only one that needs to.

Decent people are easy to spot, they have the same views as you do.

What isn't good for the swarm, isn't good for the bee.

It's not so much the road you travel, it's who travels with you.

Many egos hide their hideousness in humanity.

Humanity thrives on tradition, and traditions are ruled by the dead.

One man's food is another man's poison.

I live not in myself, I am a portion of what is around me.

The cloud that bursts wets the whole neighbourhood.

When a litter snuggles in together, they all keep warm.

Friendship

Forget it, I'm not that lonely!

Friendship is God's apology for the family he gave you.

A real friend says nice things about you behind your back.

We meet by chance, but become friends by choice.

Turn over an excuse, and friendship begins to squirm underneath.

Can I get you anything? Tea, coffee, hats, coats?

If I didn't have so many friends, I wouldn't have so many problems.

Solitude is being your own crowd.

Some people stay longer in an hour than others do in a month.

A guest sees more in a day than his host sees in a year.

Friendship is visiting friends, but not too often.

A friend walks in when others walk out.

Fish and guests stink after three days.

True friendship is seen through the heart and not the eyes.

The less they're used, the longer friends last.

Better to be alone than in bad company.

Please don't strain our friendship by asking me to do something for you.

A patched up friendship never lasts.

The friends you make in prosperity are the ones you lose in adversity.

The door may be open but the face is shut.

Solitude is enjoying your own company, whereas loneliness is being alone.

In prosperity our friends know us, in adversity we know our friends.

A new friend is about as trustworthy as an old enemy.

Solitude gives us a glimpse of our own character.

No-one is so rich that he can afford to lose a friend.

A friend should bear his friend's infirmities.

Many acquaintances, few friends.

One friend is much, two are many, and three hardly seem possible.

Some friends are merely acquaintances, and some acquaintances are new friends.

A friend to all is a friend to none.

Before borrowing, decide which you need more, the friend or the money.

It's amazing how long it takes to get rid of someone who really can't stay.

The essence of true friendship is to make allowances for another's lapses.

A friend in need is a pest indeed.

Old friends help us grow old gracefully and new friends keep us young.

The best mirror in which to see yourself is a friend.

Everyone needs at least two friends, one to talk about, and one to talk to.

True friendship is like good health, you don't miss it till it's gone.

Live so that your friends never have to defend you.

The strongest friendships are formed in mutual adversity.

Don't talk to strangers unless you know them well.

Be polite to everyone, but friendly only to a few.

A friend knows all about you, and still likes you.

Of all the plagues, the worst is a candid friend.

Don't seek approval, you find your best friends in defeat.

No matter how worthless someone is, his friendship is better than his hate.

Neighbours

My wife never knows what she wants until the neighbours get it.

If only the fence was a little shorter, or I was a little taller.

Don't laugh at your neighbours, you're probably entertaining them too.

I'm just being neighbourly, but they can't mind their own damn business.

Keeping up with the neighbours is a billion dollar a year industry.

Neighbours are people who buy things they don't need at prices they can't afford, to impress people they don't like.

A good neighbour increases the value of your home.

If your neighbours like you, you're probably a good person.

The state of the neighbourhood reflects the state of the nation.

The gums best understand the teeth's business.

If you own the land, cultivate the neighbours.

When extremes meet, let it be on common ground.

Sleeping Beauty obviously had quieter neighbours than we've got.

If you can't keep up with the Jones's, drag them down to your level.

If you want the truth about your family, ask a neighbour.

Nothing illuminates like an angry neighbour.

A hedge between keeps friendship green.

Love thy neighbour, but don't get caught.

Nothing makes you more tolerant of noise than being invited to your next door neighbour's party.

A wise fox never robs his neighbour's hen roost.

Good fences make good neighbours.

It's cheaper to drag the Jones' down to your level.

They borrow everything, but they never take a hint.

It's discouraging trying to be a good neighbour in a bad neighbourhood.

Mix with the neighbours if you want to know what your kids are up to.

Love your neighbour, but choose your neighbourhood carefully.

Everyone designs his own life, but the neighbours oversee the construction.

Pray for your neighbours, don't prey on them.

I'm better than my neighbours, at least I don't have to live next door to me.

A man with no front garden looks forlorn.

A bird never soils its own nest.

You can fool the devil, but you can't fool the neighbours.

It's easier to love the whole of humanity, and hate the guy next door.

We would have been a lot better off financially if it hadn't been for our neighbours' extravagances.

The only people who listen when you rant and rave are the neighbours.

Don't criticise your neighbours, look who they live next door to.

You can love your neighbour, but that doesn't mean you have to rush over every time you see him.

We can survive without friends, but not without neighbours.

A neighbour's drains are always worse than yours, and his garden is always better.

Better a near neighbour than a distant relative.

How do you suppose salesmen know the owner/occupier lives here?

We honour ourselves through our neighbour's shame.

Men

Not all men are the same, they have different faces so that women can tell them apart.

Men invented language to satisfy their deep need to complain.

God created man to make the angels laugh.

If the world was a logical place, men would ride side saddle.

If I wasn't born male, I might have grown up without a single toy.

This isn't a beer gut, it's a fuel tank for a love machine.

Man was made at the end of the week, when God was tired.

The ideal man is any widow's first husband.

The thoughtlessness of the male evokes the vindictiveness of the female.

The more dangerous a man is, the more attractive it makes him.

When men meet, they listen. When women meet, they look.

Man is the smallest part of nothing, and the greatest part of everything.

Real men don't wear plastic aprons.

Of course women are foolish, they were made to match men.

All men are born equal, but some get over it.

If only Adam had died with all his ribs.

Woman is the most dangerous of all man's toys.

By the time a man finally understands women, he's lost interest in them.

Most men have the sensitivity of a medieval dentist.

Men have the aspirations of creators, and the characteristics of brutes.

You don't have to twist a man's arm, you can simply wrap him around your little finger.

I like men to be men, strong and childish.

A man's age commands respect, a woman's age commands tact.

Words are women, deeds are men.

Men live by forgetting, women thrive on memories.

When humanity leapt from monkey to man, men didn't jump far enough.

A man is what his mother made him.

Men age earlier, but they wrinkle later.

Man is the head, but the woman turns it.

Man is nature's sole mistake

He's one of the nicest little old ladies I've ever met.

The older men get, the younger their wives get.

Man is a biped without feathers.

When Adam was introduced to Eve, he turned over a new leaf.

Love enters a man through his eyes.

He who has one woman has all women, and he who has all women has no woman.

Men are children of a larger growth.

Men make laws, women make manners.

If it's a man's world, it's because women don't want it.

If men had babies, maternity leave would be in the bill of rights.

The more I see of men, the more I like dogs.

Man is a map of misery.

Men with pierced ears are better prepared for marriage because they've bought expensive jewellery and experienced pain.

He knows all about women, mostly what he's been able to pick up.

Women like quiet men because they think they're listening.

Women

A woman with PMS and ESP is a bitchy know it all.

There are only two ways to handle a woman, but nobody knows either of them.

This isn't a hot flush, it's a power surge.

Women are bad at mathematics. They can't tell how old they are, how fast they were going, or how long it takes them to get ready.

Menstruation is the weeping of a disappointed uterus.

The years a woman subtracts from her own age are never wasted, they get added to other women's ages.

If you want to know why they're called the opposite sex, just express an opinion.

Intuition is the instinct that tells a woman she is right, whether she is or not.

Never trust something that bleeds for a week and does not die.

Women count their age from marriage, not from birth.

A woman whose face shows laughter lines has dated a lot of clowns.

There are only two kinds of women, goddesses and doormats.

A woman should never be accurate about her age, it looks so calculating.

Not all women nag, some aren't married.

Tears are a woman's weapon.

I like to look at women, but I wouldn't want to own one.

Never trust a woman who tells you her age. She can't keep anything secret.

Women are too imaginative to have much power of reasoning.

Women comfort men, but if it wasn't for women, men wouldn't need comforting.

Man has his will, but woman has her way.

Because is a woman's reason.

If only I could fall into her arms without falling into her hands.

I have an irrational fear of women, even thought I know they can't hurt me.

Men desire successful women, so that they can manouvre them into giving it all up to raise a family.

Women have clearer minds than men because they change them more often.

Men are the reason women don't love one another.

A woman's desire for revenge outlasts all her other emotions.

A woman's place is in the wrong.

Every woman is wrong until she cries.

Woman is a calamity, but every house must have its curse.

Women, at best, are bad.

God counts a woman's tears.

I'm glad I'm a woman, otherwise I might be tempted to marry one.

The trouble with women is men.

A man without a woman is like a neck without a pain in it.

A woman is like a gun. Don't fool with it.

Women make conversation, men speak.

A woman's guess is more accurate than a man's certainty.

Men are more attracted by what a woman doesn't mind, than by her mind.

A woman is never as old as her best friend says she is.

Just because you understand one woman, don't assume you understand them all.

For every woman who ever made a fool out of a man, there's another woman who made a man out of a fool.

Status

Fame

Great fleas have little fleas upon their backs to bite them.

In case of accident, call a reporter.

The greatest king on the biggest throne still sits on his own backside.

Some are born great, some achieve greatness, and some have terrific agents.

Glory may be fleeting, but obscurity is forever.

She is a former has-been.

A flea doesn't care whether he lives on a giant or a midget.

Today's rising star is tomorrow's black hole in space.

A celebrity is someone who works hard to have his indifference to public notice universally recognised.

I don't care what they say about me, as long as it isn't true.

Meeting a celebrity in person is always disappointing, because the bad bits can't be edited out.

Obscurity is the refuge of the incompetent.

There is nothing so ordinary as the desire to be famous.

There are many paths to the top of the mountain, but the view is the same for everyone.

Today a fire, tomorrow ashes.

Anonymity represents a liberating phenomenon.

No man is a hero to his undertaker.

I am perfectly happy to believe that nobody likes me except the public.

If you're the one on the stage, who else would they throw eggs at?

The odds are a million to one, against my being one in a million.

It's better to be looked over than to be overlooked.

Better a little fire to warm us than a great one to burn us.

Blessed is he whose fame does not obscure his truth.

The highest tower must have deep foundations or the wind will blow it over.

Legend is a matter of dying at the right time.

Fame is getting onto your own pedestal.

Fame is when you're well known by people who don't know you.

Put a pig in the limelight and he won't grunt.

Fame is a magnifying glass.

Every artist loves applause.

I scorn applause, and yet I dread criticism.

Fame kicks loyalty out.

Lean on approval, and it becomes a bed of thorns.

He is the most over rated under rated celebrity.

Pity those who are so famous that their personal tragedies are public knowledge.

Cheese is milk's leap toward immortality.

His name is greater than his ability.

Fools admire, but sensible people merely approve.

JFK was an American tear duct.

Fame should be the result and not the motive for our actions.

Everybody knows you, you know nobody.

Notoriety is different from fame, believe it or not.

Freedom

Before you can escape, you have to realise you're a prisoner.

Better to starve free than to be a fat slave.

The demanding minority have more freedoms than the silent majority.

Speak up, or shut up.

Your freedom to swing your arms stops at the tip of my nose.

Freedom is an abstract concept.

You can measure the freedom of a slave by the length of his chains.

Freedom is a hard core of agreement, held together by individual differences.

Freedom is lost little by little, never all at once.

Man will never be free until the last king is strangled with the entrails of the last priest.

We are the slaves of our obligations.

Sometimes a good crutch is better than a bad foot.

It is the process of setting man free from man.

Liberty does not come from the government.

Freedom is an abstract concept.

None are more hopelessly enslaved than those who think they are free.

Freedom is an optimistic view of pessimistic people.

There's a big difference between freedom of speech and loose talk.

You may use your freedom as you please, but allow me to use mine too.

We have to endure most from those we are most dependent upon.

Freedom is a state of mind. Even birds are chained to the sky.

If you were born to command, you will find it difficult to obey.

Freedom has a thousand charms that slaves, however contented, will never know.

My chains may be gold, but they still restrict my movements.

The dwarf on the giant's shoulders can see the furthest of the two.

Four walls do not a prison make, nor iron bars a cage.

Freedom is safety to say what you think, even if others don't agree with you.

Freedom is not measured by privileges, but by responsibilities.

Too much freedom has the same effect as too little freedom.

The only difference between the dark ages and the present, is that the minority now makes the rules the majority have to abide by.

Freedom gives us the right to be our own oppressors.

You have to fight for your freedom, and war erodes freedom.

When a prisoner escapes, the last thing on his mind is where his next meal will come from.

Our only freedom is to discipline ourselves.

To maintain freedom, you need to guard your enemies against oppression.

Freedom of speech is being able to say what you think without thinking.

Freedom is imagination's most valuable possession.

Freedom is the right to mismanage your own affairs.

A prisoner soon grows accustomed to his cell.

Freedom of speech means allowing every donkey the right to bray.

Freedom of speech gives you the right to speak freely, but it does not require me to obey what you command.

Poverty

To darn socks is to premeditate poverty.

The trouble with being poor is that it takes up so much of your time.

Thank God there's no disgrace in being poor, there are enough disadvantages without having to worry about that too.

A rich man is a poor man with money.

Just when you're about to make ends meet, someone moves the ends.

One man's loss is another man's new umbrella.

Big mouthfuls often choke.

In a poor country, wealth is something to be ashamed of.

Very few people can afford to be poor.

Even if I died tomorrow, I still wouldn't have enough to live on for the rest of my life.

If money talks, all it ever says to me is goodbye.

Necessity relieves us of the embarrassment of choice.

When you almost make both ends meet, something always breaks.

Maybe a poor man can't always afford meat, but a rich man can't always digest it.

Poverty is punishment for a crime you didn't commit.

We choose according to our needs.

Offer a starving man money, and he will sell you the last of his food.

Poverty commands pity, but beggars incite anger.

Ask your wallet what you can afford.

Poverty is a state of mind, but only to a philosopher with a full stomach.

If the rich could pay the poor to die for them, the poor would finally make a decent living.

I have progressed from needy to deprived, from underprivileged to disadvantaged, and I'm still poor.

Poverty hides, but wealth is conspicuous.

May poverty always be at least a day's march behind you.

If the poor didn't grow food, the rich would have nothing to eat except money.

For every talent that poverty has stimulated, it has destroyed a hundred.

A beggar can never be bankrupt.

Inflation is making it twice as hard to live beyond our means than it did five years ago.

The debt set.

We only boast about poverty when we have overcome it.

The only vehicle we can almost afford is the supermarket trolley.

Until debt us do part.

Poverty rises as society advances.

The working class are becoming the new poor.

A small loan makes a debtor, a big one an enemy.

Poverty is worse in a wealthy country.

To be poor is a sin the rich cannot forgive.

Poverty is not so much having nothing, as craving much.

Fight poverty, throw stones at beggars.

You lose your manners when you are poor.

Poverty comes from God, but filth doesn't.

Poverty is when there is too much month at the end of your salary.

Poverty is when you try to satisfy many needs with few resources.

Poverty is no disgrace, but it is damn inconvenient.

Wealth

As privileged as a politician.

Only the very wealthy are rich enough to treat money with the contempt it deserves.

I'd give anything to be a philanthropist.

To be stinking rich is what makes people effluent.

You can't have everything, where would you put it all?

Money is the root of all evil, and the ultimate blessing.

It's not a sin to be rich, it's a bloody miracle.

I've been rich and I've been poor, and rich is better.

When he lost his fortune, she declared her undying love, even if she never saw him again.

Truth whispers, money shouts.

No man owns a fortune, it owns him.

When I was young I thought money was everything, and I was right.

Wealth is moral. It only allows those who love it to have it.

The love of money is the root of all evil. Therefore love is bad, money is all.

Inheritance is the money that men make, that lives on after them.

Money is the root of all evil, but it's the one we all root for.

It's impossible to overdo luxury.

Only the brave deserve the beautiful, but only the rich can afford them.

The best way to accumulate wealth is to ignore your debts.

All heiresses are beautiful.

Help me to money, and I'll help myself to friends.

Never kiss a gift horse in the mouth.

Only when the rich are ill do they feel the impotence of wealth.

A full cup should be carried carefully.

A rich man and his daughter are soon parted.

Life is a bubble and cash keeps it afloat.

A rich man will never know the joy of paying off the last instalment.

There's no reason to stir if you were born with a silver spoon in your mouth.

Rich men cover their faults with money so they aren't obvious.

Maybe money can't buy happiness, but it allows me to be miserable in luxury.

Insurance keeps us poor so that we can die rich.

Money is that elusive something that rushes past us on its way to the government.

You need money to make money.

Wealth is what keeps rich people in debt.

You may labour for the wealthy, but your reward will be small.

Rich men have no faults.

Respectable means rich, decent means poor.

You have to be rich to be able to enjoy the simple things in life that are free.

Prosperous times are filled with friends.

Better to die like a beggar than to live like one.

You can see what God thinks of money by the people he gives most of it to.

Too much money makes us vulgar, too little makes us coarse.

A fool and his money get the pick of the crop.

Never invest in anything that needs a veterinarian.

Welfare

It's everyone else's job to support me.

There's nothing wrong with work, but it takes up too much of my time.

When you're getting a free ride, you don't care how far it is to town.

Welfare is the government's attempt to distribute poverty equally.

Support the rich, they provide welfare for the poor.

It's better to have been on the dole briefly, than never to have loafed at all.

It's not that I don't want to work, but my spare time is too precious to waste job hunting.

Welfare gives me time to make the most of the hours I need to feel depressed.

Those who won't work give those who can't find work a bad name.

I can cope without the essentials, but don't deprive me of my luxuries.

The government keeps training me for jobs I'll never do, but at least I have more confidence.

The rich get richer, and the poor get welfare.

Hard work never hurt anyone who paid someone else to do it.

I resent being treated like the despicable layabout I really am.

I realise now that the ambitions I once had weren't worth having anyway.

The dole is the reward the government gives you for not working.

The poor man's happiness is purchased from the rich man's purse.

I have tasted everything, and there is nothing so sweet as being given without have to resort to begging.

Where everyone stinks, you can't smell anyone.

I wrote to myself threatening to stop my dole payments if I didn't look for a job, and I got a defiant reply.

God helps those who help themselves, and the government helps those who don't.

Welfare is society's approval of the perpetual holiday.

Even if I have nothing to offer, you still have to share what you have with me.

Welfare is when the government takes from those who work, and gives it to those who don't.

The mere thought of looking for work is work, for which I should be paid.

Welfare is when the government employs large numbers of unemployed.

We take welfare for gratis.

Welfare is socialism for the unemployed.

It's not about having nothing, it's about wanting it all for nothing.

The government sends me mail just to make me feel important.

Unemployment takes the worry out of being late for work.

Most of my faults are not my fault.

Why should I get up early and use public transport for your benefit? I'm already getting all the benefits I want.

If you won't work according to your ability, starve according to your income.

All I want is the opportunity to prove that money wouldn't have made me happy anyway.

He who considers work beneath him, is above doing anything.

If only I could be well respected, without having to work.

If it wasn't for the dole, poverty would have forced me to find work.

If only I had fewer needs, and the government did more to satisfy them.

The function of welfare is to raise suffering to a higher level.

Success

Ambition

Ambition is the delusion that you're destined for greater things.

Dead fish stink, but they rise to the surface.

So much ambition, so little ability.

If you want to keep your head when everyone else is losing theirs, take charge of the guillotine.

Goals are dreams with deadlines.

It's lonely at the top, but you live better.

I wish I either had less ambition or more get up and go.

Anyone can stand in the gutter and look at the stars.

Ambition is the ability to make stepping stones out of stumbling blocks.

I sat down and worked out where I stood, instead of sitting on the fence.

If you're thinking anyway, think big.

An ass laden down with gold rises faster.

Shit floats to the top.

When your dreams turn to dust, vacuum.

Nothing is beneath you if it takes you in the direction of your greatest ambition.

The wind blows hardest on the tallest trees.

Behind every able man there are other able men waiting to take his place.

Don't wait for someone to give it to you, take it.

Life will not kill the dream I dream.

Even if you don't qualify to be a giant, it doesn't mean you have to be content to be a pygmy.

If you're satisfied with what you are, don't aim higher.

A man with burning ambition rarely gets fired.

Ambition is dreaming about what you want and working towards it.

Ambition is conceit wearing its best outfit.

Ambition creeps as well as soars.

A man may be so much of everything that he becomes nothing of anything.

Rise like a rocket, fall like a stick.

Never despise those on the lower rungs of the ladder. They're still climbing.

A man's reach should always exceed his grasp.

If I have seen further, it is by standing on the shoulders of giants.

He left to set the world on fire but had to come home for matches.

A man is the sun of his own creation.

There is always room at the top.

Ambition is the desire to over-achieve.

Watch out for ambition. It can get you into a whole lot of hard work.

The wisest men follow their own direction.

Ambition is the desire to always want more than you can accomplish.

A man cannot be comfortable without his own approval.

I am not burdened by power. I love it.

Ambition is the initiative that begins the echo.

It's not how high you go, but how you get there.

Audacity

Let's agree not to step on one another's toes, said the ant to the elephant.

Nothing ventured, nothing stuffed up.

He who hesitates has lost the parking spot.

If you can crack the shell, the world is your oyster.

If you soar like an eagle, you attract hunters.

You've got to take the bull by the teeth.

Don't be a carbon copy. Make your own impression.

Nine out of ten attempts fail. That's why you have to try ten times harder.

If you must travel on the Titanic, book the presidential suite.

Only the bold get to the top.

In a strong world, you have to be strong.

Big shots are little shots that kept on shooting.

Enjoy what you can. Endure what you must.

Audacity is the ability to think and act outside the square you live in.

Walk and the world walks with you, run and you run alone.

Don't beg if you're capable of theft.

Before a mouse laughs at a cat, he makes sure he's near a hole.

Don't be afraid to take a large step. You can't cross a chasm in two leaps.

Professional courtesy allows him to swim through shark-infested waters in safety.

Audacity is when you murder your parents and ask the court for leniency because you're an orphan.

We never put our best foot forward before the other one lands in hot water.

The best form of defence is offence.

Audacity is pinning badges on frankfurters and selling them as police dogs.

If you want to put yourself on the map, publish your own map.

When the water rises, the boat also rises.

A fly is the greatest symbol of audacity.

Audacity supplements courage, hesitation stimulates fear.

Blessed are the meek, for they shall pay the inheritance tax.

Whatever you dream you can do, begin it now.

Audacity achieves because it has power and magic.

Never throw rocks at a crocodile until you've crossed the river.

A hawk flies higher than a canary.

Audacity is knowing how far to go when you go too far.

The people I respect the most think they're immortal and society is eternal.

Ambition is the last refuge of the failure.

Go out on a limb-that's where the fruit is.

Small minds are the first to condemn ideas that they could not conceive.

The weak in courage must be strong in cunning.

If you want the cubs, you have to go into the tiger's den.

A good archer isn't famous for his arrows but for his aim.

Audacity is knowing how stupid your opponent is.

They can't get your goat if they don't know where you keep it tethered.

He who watches the wind will not sow, and he who watches the clouds will not reap.

Fate loves the fearless.

Keep a diary and one day it will keep you.

Leadership

If you're not the lead dog in the sled team, the scenery never changes.

It's hard to look up to a leader who keeps his ear to the ground.

The speed of the leader sets the pace of the pack.

Ah well, I am their leader, I might as well follow them.

It's easier to raise an army than it is to find a general.

Leadership is being there early to see who gets in late.

Any man surrounded by dwarves looks like a giant.

Leadership isn't about choosing the winning side, it's the ability to unite both sides.

Don't follow me. I'm lost too.

The longer the line, the worse the usher.

A manager is someone who gets someone else to pass the buck.

You can always tell a leader, but you can't tell him much.

A leader can face the music, even when he doesn't like the tune.

Good leaders are scarce. You have to follow your own nose.

A leader is a dealer in hope.

It's better to follow well than to lead badly.

So many sheep, so few good shepherds.

Leadership is not position, it's action.

The only training for leadership is leadership.

Follow me, I'm right behind you.

Management is what makes it difficult to get ahead.

Before you cry *Forward,* decide which direction to take.

Everyone is looking for someone to follow.

A leader marches like a soldier, but dreams like a visionary.

Some leaders take great pains and give them to others.

To be powerful, you need a genius for organisation.

You can either rule or be honest, but you can't do both at the same time.

In every work of genius we recognise the thoughts we never acted on.

A leader uses no as the starting point of his negotiations.

Whenever a new leader commands, we begin to value his predecessor.

Uncertainty is part of taking charge.

A good leader's followers will gladly pursue him over the precipice.

Use thoughtful words to make convincing arguments.

A man is never as great at home as he is abroad.

A leader is someone who can pat another on the back without making him fall flat on his face.

The function of leadership is to produce leaders, not followers.

Nice guys don't even get a chance to start.

Don't follow anyone until you know whom he's behind.

Leadership isn't speed, it's the direction and style with which you arrive.

People are more easily led than driven.

There are too many chiefs and not enough Indians.

No-one sees what a leader aimed at, only what he hit.

A leader is someone who only emerges from meetings to sign letters.

The fault is not the rulers, it belongs to those who allow themselves to be underlings.

Where you stand depends on where you sit.

Success

I came, I saw, I kicked arse.

Success is an achievement that covers a multitude of failures.

An obstacle is something you see when you take your eye off the goal.

Success is the ability to make money faster than you can create debt.

If you run into a brick wall, climb it.

Success is the ability to get on well with those above you, and to get ahead of those around you.

Some people confuse movement with effort.

Success is not the ability to get on with people, it's the ability to get ahead of them.

People with goals succeed because they know where they're going.

Never look back unless you plan to retreat.

If at first you don't succeed, give up. There's no point in making a fool of yourself.

Success goes to the head, failure goes to the heart.

The road to success is filled with women pushing their husbands along.

High hopes and low overheads.

Success hasn't changed him at all. He's the same old bastard he always was.

Lions ten, Christians zero.

Every successful person has had failures, but repeated failure is no guarantee of eventual success.

Details create perfection, but perfection is not a detail.

The path to success is paved with good intentions that were carried out.

What was the name of the third man on the moon?

Success is relative. The more successful you are, the more relatives you'll have.

When all else fails, read the instructions.

Don't let my success go to your head.

Success often goes straight to the mouth.

The snail reached the ark through sheer determination.

Winning isn't everything, it's the only thing.

Success has nothing to do with spontaneous combustion. You have to set yourself on fire.

Victory has many fathers, but defeat is an orphan.

Success is a matter of being in the right place at the right time.

Neither success nor failure is permanent.

If at first you don't succeed, analyse your failure before you try again.

Success is living well, laughing often, and loving much.

Winning may not be everything, but losing isn't anything.

To climb the ladder, you have to start at the bottom.

When the reviews are bad, I cry all the way to the bank.

If at first you don't succeed, at least you are learning how.

Make him an offer he can't refuse.

If you don't hear opportunity knocking, it's because you're not listening.

Success has made failures of many.

In defeat unbeatable, in victory unbearable.

Success is rewarded with higher taxes.

You can't climb the ladder of success with your hands in your pockets.

It takes about twenty years to be an overnight success.

Talent

Talent is God's gift to you. How you use it is your gift to God.

Always remember you're one of a kind, just like everybody else.

Those who want to sing will always manage to find a song.

Talent is both a gift and an obligation.

Everyone rows with the oars they have.

More men fail through a lack of purpose than through a lack of talent.

Genius does what it must, talent does what it can.

Talent is the certainty that nothing is too daunting to attempt.

Talent is what gets you to the top when the boss has no daughter.

Talent is the ability never to give up trying until you succeed.

He's not only ambidextrous, but he can write with both hands.

Talent is the ability to recognize what you're most competent at.

Any jackass can kick down a barn, but it takes a good carpenter to build one.

Talent needs effort to guide it.

Mediocrity knows nothing higher than itself, but talent instantly recognises genius.

I am easily satisfied, but only with my very best.

Some bad qualities make excellent talents.

You are only as talented as others perceive you to be.

Talent is the ability to discard what doesn't work on the path to success.

We magnify our own talents and minimise those of others.

Keep your talent hidden, and you'll never have to be insulted.

We rate men by what they finish, not by what they begin.

Specialise in what you're good at.

You're not in competition with anyone but yourself.

Talent is one part ability and nine parts determination.

If you believe you have to do it, you can.

Talent is the ability to recognise opportunity when it presents itself.

Talent merely suggests possibilities, the rest is up to you.

Genius is a talented dead man.

A weed is sometimes just a flower in disguise.

Talent isn't knowing where you want to go, it's knowing which direction to take.

The harder it is, the easier it is to achieve, because there's no competition.

Charisma is what gets us to the top when we have no talent.

The wind and the waves favour the experienced sailor.

They said it couldn't be done, but I showed them.

Some have talent but no ambition, and others have ambition, but no talent.

Talent is knowing how close to the edge you can stand without falling over.

Only mediocrity is always at its best.

It's the ability to create a need and to fill it.

Everyone has talent, but not everyone pursues it.

You have to follow your talent, even if it leads you to a dark place.

If you can't dance, vacate the floor for someone who can.

Talent is a bit of skill and a lot of confidence.

Talent calls you to your vocation.

Talent is the difference between action and reaction.

Second rate people only hire third rate people.

Superstition

Luck

Clutch your rabbit's foot for luck, but don't forget what it did for the rabbit.

The more I practice, the luckier I get.

Success is purely a matter of luck. Ask any failure.

It's unlucky to be superstitious.

Of course I believe in luck. How else do my enemies succeed?

Luck never takes her favourite unawares.

A roast chicken isn't going to fly into your mouth.

Good luck is when preparation meets opportunity.

One day my boat will come in, but with my kind of luck, I'll be at the airport.

Luck never favours the faint-hearted.

Some people run into accidents that started out happening to someone else.

Look for your luck, it won't find you on it's own.

Guide your luck while you wait for it to arrive.

The rich get ice in summer and the poor get it in winter.

Good luck knocks once, bad luck has more patience.

You can distinguish luck from ability by its duration.

Good luck makes you good, bad luck makes you bad.

A boxer will definitely win if he has a lucky horseshoe, particularly if he puts it in boxing glove.

Superstition is not an abundance of imagination, it is the total lack of any imagination.

Omens follow those who follow them.

Those who delight in luck get overthrown by destiny.

Fortune's expensive smile has to be earned.

Never mention luck to a self-made man.

Luck is a distant relative of success.

It is the mind that makes the body rich.

Good luck reaches further than long arms.

If all the world was a stage, I'd be sitting on the balcony that collapsed.

It takes skill to guide your luck.

Luck is the residue left by action.

As I was about to enter, God knelt and closed the door.

Getting caught drink driving isn't bad luck, it's a crime.

Ten minutes of good luck makes us forget all the bad luck we ever had.

When its time has come, the prey travels toward the hunter.

You will never be hanged if you were born to drown.

The cards are never well shuffled until you have a good hand.

Luck never gives, it only lends.

Everything comes at its appointed hour.

Every man is the architect of his own future.

Fate deals the hand that free will plays.

Luck is always against those who rely on it.

Some of us are moved by events, and others are mastered by them.

Not all luck is good, and not all good is luck.

We are the builders of our own fortunes.

The Supernatural

ESP stands for Essentially Stupid People.

Some things have to be believed to be seen.

Timing is the essential factor in the success of the rain dance.

Faith created many of the mountains it now needs to remove.

If you believe in fate, you don't believe in free will.

Reincarnation is making a comeback.

Meditation beats sitting around doing nothing.

A sceptic doesn't believe Siamese twins are related.

A man with a family gives fate hostages.

Only one link in the chain of destiny can be handled at a time.

Whatever limits us, we call fate.

Fate decrees that a coconut husk will float and a stone will sink.

I wouldn't have seen it if I didn't believe it.

When myth meets myth, the collision it real.

Destiny is going in search of the great perhaps.

This is the same old déjà vu all over again.

Fate leads the willing and drags the reluctant along.

Perhaps an unseen hand pushes us off the edge of the board.

You can row all you like, but you are steered by fate.

After the fountain has gone up, it comes down.

Even if fate intends for you to lose, fight it anyway.

Everyone always has a funny feeling about it, but no-one ever says so until after the event.

At tonight's annual general meeting of clairvoyants, we will be reading the minutes of next year's meeting.

It is certain that everything is uncertain.

Everyone learns geology the morning after the earthquake.

Intuition often gets the credit eavesdropping should have had.

Irrationally held truths are more harmful than reasoned errors.

Think before you think.

A hidden connection is stranger than an obvious one.

The body is the tomb of the soul.

The unknown doesn't measure up when we compare it with the known.

The best time to predict the future is after it's happened.

Heaven is where you find your rainbow, hell is where they told you it was.

Recognition of the unfamiliar is not condoned by the familiar.

Sun worshippers are prohibited from examining the detrimental properties of heat.

The soul is merely a spectator of the movements of the body.

Spiritualists like to try out new mediums.

They come out of the cracks to support belief, but they flee doubt.

Déjà moo is the feeling that you've heard this bull before.

The surest sign of intelligent life out there is that no-one has tried to contact earth.

That famous women's intuition is merely an inherent superstitious nature.

Some people are so sceptical they would even deny the existence of the unicorn.

Reality is in the eye of the beholder.

Reincarnation is when you live and die repeatedly.

Time

Future

Time stays, we pass on.

You are the future of the past.

If you wait for tomorrow, tomorrow comes. If you don't wait for tomorrow, tomorrow comes.

The future is the past entered through a different door.

The flowers of tomorrow are in the seeds of today.

Just because I'm older, doesn't mean I've changed in the past.

The future overcomes the past by devouring it.

Dream your tomorrows, but live your todays.

That tomorrow that you dreaded yesterday, is today.

That New Year's resolution is about to collide with the old year's habits.

Is tomorrow really necessary?

Nothing is eternal except eternity.

We cross our bridges before we come to them, and burn them behind us.

The best thing about the future is that it only happens a day at a time.

The future belongs to those who dare to dream.

Time is all that stops everything from happening at once.

Nothing is eternal except eternity.

I'm not afraid of tomorrow, for I have seen yesterday and today is wonderful.

If there is no struggle, there is no progress.

There's no future in the past.

We prefer familiar terrors to unknown delights.

We all want progress, but we dislike change.

Here today, gone tomorrow, lost forever.

You can build a wonderful future over a terrible past.

The present is when the future pauses before becoming the past.

The future isn't what it used to be.

While there's never time to do it properly, there's always time to do it again.

The enemy you made today might have been the person who saved your life tomorrow.

The deeper you look into the past, the more you can see of the future.

Why do we always convince ourselves that tomorrow will be better?

Today is the first day of the rest of your life.

The future never gets any closer.

It's wise to look ahead, but foolish to see further than you can look.

The future is that glorious time when we will be rich and successful.

Never is a long time, but it could be tomorrow.

So many have a bright future behind them.

And in today, tomorrow already walks.

May the happiest days of your past become the saddest days of your future.

If the chain is still swinging, the seat is still warm.

It's better to look where you're going than where you've been.

The certainties of today are the problems of tomorrow.

Warning: Dates on this calendar are closer than they appear.

I have seen the future, and it works.

Past

Time is a great teacher, but unfortunately it kills it's pupils.

Time is the rider that tames youth.

Today is what happened to yesterday.

Those who find the day too long, find life too short.

Time is not a commodity that should be measured by clocks.

These are the good old days the next generation is going to get so sick of hearing about.

Keep looking back, and you'll get a pain in the neck.

History is based on actual events, but the names haven't been changed to protect the innocent.

Let the past go.

We have all passed a lot of water since then.

Time will end all my troubles, but I don't always approve of time's methods.

Nostalgia is a thing of the past.

History is an early warning system for the present.

If you're harping about the past, you're not living the present.

Maybe the past is so attractive because it represents the known.

History is time that has grown old disgracefully.

Nothing is improbable until it moves into the past tense.

The only people who profit from the past are those involved in recording history.

History repeats itself because no-one listens.

What doesn't leave us, we leave.

The fact that what we once loved has gone does not diminish its value.

You can't water today's garden with last year's rain.

It takes a lot of time to be sentimental about the past.

We learn from history that we learn nothing from history.

Once an event has occurred, a competent historian can make it's consequences look inevitable.

Time passes and we pass with it.

We wander through the wrecks of days departed.

Longevity conquers scandal.

The whole of the past is not worth as much as today is.

Time drags us forward with itself.

History is a record of lies agreed upon by the hierarchy.

The past is always better than the future, because it's passed.

History reflects those who recorded it.

If you praise the past, you blame the present.

Forget what has been and make the most of what is coming.

We are tomorrow's past.

History carries living memories to the future.

Our happiest times always lie in the past, but that's because we were younger then.

The past shows us what mistakes we are going to make.

Keep travelling, there are no yesterday's on the road.

History is a biography of great men and women, and we all know how accurate biographies are.

History tells us William Tell shot an arrow through an apple while standing on his son's head.

Patience

God grant me patience, but please hurry.

Everything comes to he who hustles while he waits.

Take your time, but hurry up.

Beware the fury of a patient man.

With patience, a mulberry leaf becomes a silk gown.

Every minute starts an hour.

A wound heals by degrees.

The best way to kill time is to work it to death.

Patience is a flower that doesn't grow in every garden.

The greatest disadvantage of hurry is that it takes so long.

Patience is a good nag, but she'll bolt.

Patience melts an ice cream before you've licked it.

I waited for hours and no-one arrived, so quite early on, I knew you were late.

I only count the sunny hours.

Although patience may be a tired mare, yet will she plod.

Patience comes to those who wait for it.

Patience is a bitter plant, but it has a sweet fruit.

You invite a new injury if you bear the old one patiently.

Little drops of water wear down big stones.

There's always enough time for failure.

A day old chick won't provide roast chicken by nightfall.

No-one remembers how long it took you to do it, only how well you did it.

Not so miserable suffering, as pleased with patience.

Patience accomplishes, hurry ruins.

Those who kill time ultimately find it is stronger than they are.

You only have to endure to conquer.

Be as long as you like, but don't dawdle.

Little by little does the trick.

What's the point of praying for patience? I need it right now.

And not before time either.

He who preaches patience never knew pain.

Patience is the inability to be decisive.

No matter how much the river winds, it finds the sea eventually.

You can delay, but time won't.

Patience may be a virtue, but it will never help a rooster lay an egg.

Impatient people always arrive too late.

Sometimes the day ahead seems longer than the year ahead.

If you can't endure it conveniently, endure it patiently.

Patience is the ability to wait without worrying.

Be patient my soul, you have suffered more than this.

Patience is laziness disguised as a virtue.

To everything there is a season, and a time to every purpose under heaven.

I will be spontaneous tomorrow.

Only a vulture waits for its dinner to die.

Abused patience turns to fury.

The problem with being patient is that people think you don't understand the problem.

Punctuality

The reason for the rush is the delay.

Even when I'm punctual, the meeting is delayed until the latecomers arrive.

You're not actually late until you arrive.

Better a child who gets home late, than a late child.

You snooze, you lose.

Don't rush me. I've only got one other speed, and it's slower than this.

If you're there before it's over, you're on time.

If you can delay it long enough, the need for it may disappear.

Imagination waits with you when someone is late.

It's not the time you put in, it's what you put in the time.

I hate friends who arrive too late to help.

If it weren't for the last minute, nothing would ever be finished on time.

Being late isn't about time, it's about lack of respect.

Ever since I told her I was a stickler for punctuation, she's never been late.

Better never than late.

Punctuality is a sign of better times.

Time specialises in alterations.

When you save time, you get it back with interest.

A rock given at the right time is better than gold given at the wrong time.

If it's worth doing, it's worth doing late.

On the other hand, the early worm gets eaten.

Going slower doesn't prevent your arrival.

This is the earliest you've been late for a long time.

The speed of time is infinite.

Better three hours too soon than one minute too late.

Make time while time is, for time will away.

A split second is the interval between the lights turning green, and the car behind honking at you.

If I hadn't rushed to catch the bus, I wouldn't have had to wait so long for the next one.

To one who waits, a minute seems like an hour.

Nothing is as inevitable as a mistake whose time has come.

Time flies, and drags us with it.

The problem with getting there on time is that there's no-one there to appreciate it.

Why can't trouble come later?

Nothing weighs more heavily on a relationship that the lack of punctuality.

There are no birds in last year's nest.

Never put off till tomorrow what you could have done today.

Punctuality is the soul of business.

Initial effort is in proportion to the time allotted. As time diminishes, effort increases.

Better late than before anyone invites you.

Punctuality is the virtue of the boring.

My time has not yet come.

Who waits for the right time, loses time.

While waiting, we examine the faults of those for whom we wait.

Those who live closest always arrive last.

Vices

Drinking

I'm not so think as you drunk I am.

Let me slip out of these wet clothes and into a dry martini.

I'm not an alcoholic. They go to meetings.

I know exactly how much I can drink before I get drunk, but I always seem to get drunk before I reach my quota.

Alcohol has been helping ugly people have sex for hundreds of years.

One tequila, two tequila, three tequila, floor.

I am drunk and you are ugly, but in the morning, I will be sober.

Wine is proof that God loves us and wants us to be happy.

Twenty-four beers in a carton, twenty-four hours in a day. Coincidence?

God made beer. In God we trust.

I'd rather sleep with a sober cannibal than a drunken Christian.

What contemptible scoundrel took the cork out of my lunch?

I drink to forget I drink.

You can keep the house and the children, but I'll fight you for custody of the port.

Heineken refreshes the parts other beers can't reach.

I only drink to make my friends more interesting.

There's no cure for the mourning after.

Better to pay the publican than the doctor.

Wine in, truth out.

I'd rather have a bottle in front of me than a full frontal lobotomy.

Drink brandy if you want courage. Beer only makes you piss.

Booze creates employment for publicans, police, doctors and undertakers.

If the bar is moving, chances are you're being carried out.

A cask of wine can work more miracles than a saint can.

As they brew, so shall we drink.

Don't complain about the beer, one day you too will be old and weak.

Heavy drinkers are more likely to go to heaven than non-drinkers, because they pass out, and when they've passed out, they are without sin.

Drink, and find out where you came from, and why.

If the barman suddenly appears blurred, it's because you're seeing him through the bottom of an empty glass, and you need a refill.

If I'm not allowed to drink and drive, how come I need to produce a driver's licence to buy alcohol?

She said she'd leave me if I didn't stop drinking. I'm going to miss that woman.

If the opposite wall now has a fluorescent light on it, you've probably fallen over.

A toast to the thirst that is yet to come.

I don't drink water because fish fornicate in it.

If prayer doesn't help, turn to booze.

We keep alcohol in the home for purely medicinal purposes, but I'm constantly ill.

What the sober man has in his heart, the drunk has on his lips.

A woman drove me to drink, and I never even thanked her.

There are more old drunks than old doctors.

Work is the curse of the drinking class.

Gambling

I bet you I could stop gambling right now if I wanted to.

May the odds be with you.

Daddy loved the zoo, especially the horse that came in at thirty-to-one.

If gambling is a disease, why can't I claim my losses as medical expenses?

I love sick horses. Mind you, I never realise they're sick until I bet on them.

You're not going places, you're being taken.

I BACKED A HORSE AT TWENTY-FIVE TO ONE....

AND IT CAME IN AT FOUR-THIRTY!

Those who can afford to gamble don't need the money, and those that need the money can't afford to gamble.

A long run of good luck is a sure sign of bad luck.

Never give a sucker an even break.

It's not the hand you're dealt, it's how you play it.

Horse sense is what stops horses from betting on people.

The more you lose in strip poker, the more you have to show for it.

Heads you win, tails I lose.

Winners joke, losers act serious.

The luckiest gambler is the one with the strength to walk away.

A racehorse is the only animal in the world that can take hundreds of people for a ride at the same time.

Don't bet more than you can afford to lose.

A slot machine is a steel trap which captures gullible humans.

You should play fairly, especially if you already have the winning hand.

Cards were supposed to amuse us, not enslave us.

Put up or shut up.

This is a vice that destroys mighty men.

Never bet on a loser because you think his luck is about to change.

Gambling stems from man's secret desire to outsmart horses, fish and women.

Don't play with scared money.

Boredom creates more gamblers than greed does.

You can't make a fast buck out of a slow horse

Let him who loses all die a beggar, unpitied.

The winner's joy is the loser's sorrow.

If you're clanging your horseshoes, you won't hear opportunity knocking.

If I were trained as a tailor, nudity would prevail.

He only gambles for fun. So far he's laughed his way through a house, a car and a boat.

He bet on a horse everyone said would walk it, and it did.

Don't bet on horses, bet on jockeys.

Gambling is taking money from people who guessed wrong.

The stock market is the most respectable form of gambling.

Blessed are those who can give without remembering, and receive without forgetting.

The horse was so slow the jockey died of starvation.

My son is only two, and he can already count from ace to king.

Gambling is when you go broke trying to get rich.

It's not horse racing that needs reform, it's the humans around it.

Gambling is the surest way of getting nothing for something.

No-one has more faith than the man playing a slot machine.

Bad Habits

As soon as I stopped smoking I started fuming.

Why do you think they call it dope?

I read so much about the dangers of smoking that I had to give up reading.

Every habit keeps an excuse handy.

Smoking is God's way of saying you have too much money.

Well, I've been smoking for years and I'm not addicted yet.

Get thee down. Be thou funky.

Tobacco Road runs into a dead end.

A slave to his own body has many masters.

Been there, done that, can't remember most of it.

If God had intended us to smoke, our ears would be chimneys.

Smoking doesn't increase the death rate, it is still one per person.

Self-respect grows from the ability to say no to yourself.

The first thing you lose when you give up smoking is your sense of humour.

Better living, through chemistry.

A bartender is a pharmacist with liquid stocks.

Giving up smoking is the easiest thing in the world. I've done it thousands of times.

Nothing succeeds like excess.

When used as directed, smoking kills.

Those who abstain carry their repressed desires around with them.

Dope is a substitute for hope.

I'm not gullible. What's wrong with wrapping a dehydrated leaf in paper, lighting it up and inhaling it, even if it makes me cough?

Better to limit your desires than to try to satisfy them.

Cancer cures smoking.

Smokers don't have a higher mortality rate, it's only the time factor that differs.

Abstinence is better than mastering your pleasure.

Index